SPECIAL THANKS TO THE JOHN S. AND JAMES L. KNIGHT FOUNDATION FOR THE FINANCIAL SUPPORT THAT CONTINUES TO FUND THE PICTURE EDITING DIVISION OF THE MOUNTAIN WORKSHOPS. THIS BOOK IS A RESULT OF THAT SUPPORT.

MUHLENBERG COUNTY, KENTUCKY

The 1999 Mountain Workshops

ADDITIONAL THANKS TO THE COMMUNITIES OF CENTRAL CITY, GREENVILLE AND MUHLENBERG COUNTY IN CENTRAL KENTUCKY. THANKS FOR LETTING US SPEND TIME WITH YOU.

COVER PHOTO BY TOM LEININGER
ABOVE PHOTO BY TERRENCE JAMES

WHERE PARADISE LAY

1

Where paradise lay
and the faces of these times...

Cover photo •
Lisa Oliver and her son, William, admire Jennifer Crowder's new daughter, Halley Lynn Hines. Oliver is Crowder's younger sister. Crowder's other daughter, Kaitlyn, looks on. Haley was born Tuesday, Oct. 5, 1999, at the Muhlenberg Community Hospital.

PHOTO BY
TOM LEININGER

Page 1 photo •
Betty Groves and sister Linda Croft clown around while having a yard sale at Croft's home in Greenville.

PHOTO BY
TERRENCE JAMES

Back cover photo •
The Whitehouse children and a neighbor roll a bale of hay near their Bremen home. Country living means a forest for a back yard and space for the Pentecostal family with 11 children living at home.

PHOTO BY
SARAH REINGEWIRTZ

FOR GENERATIONS

when people looked at Muhlenberg County, Kentucky, they usually saw only one thing: coal. The thick seams beneath the ground were torn open and tons of black rock were dug out and shipped out, making Muhlenberg at one time the richest mineral-producing county in the nation. Families assumed that their destiny and prosperity were as fixed as the stars. Coal was king.

With the collapse of the coal market and closing of the mines in the '70s and '80s, residents of Muhlenberg were forced to adapt, to tough it out, to improvise, to endure. The deeper, truer seams of their lives, the ones based on faith, family and neighborliness, came into view. Character was bedrock.

For a week in October 1999, about 50 photojournalists came to look at Muhlenberg County. What they saw was a multitude of things – hard work, hard play, a birth, a fire, big families, broken families, hands clasped in friendship and in prayer, and even some coal mining.

The shooters gathered for the 22nd annual Mountain Workshop, sponsored by the photojournalism program at Western Kentucky University in Bowling Green. In one week's time, the young photojournalists would undergo an initiation into their profession: to find subjects, win their trust, look beneath the surface, and then step back and make pictures that show things deep and fresh. None of it would have worked without the hospitality of the Muhlenberg folk. They gave and the students gave back.

Each morning the photojournalists fanned out from their base at the Wendell H. Ford Training Center, a National Guard facility built on the reclaimed grounds of the famous River Queen mine. They drove the back roads with Sheriff Jerry Mayhugh, followed the zigs and zags of high school tailback Joey Mercer, sweated under the hot autumn sun at a tobacco farm with migrant workers from Mexico, looked inside a day care center and an explosives factory, went 240 feet down into a coal mine with Shirley McLemore and 500 feet high with ex-miner Rodney Douglas in a plane he had fixed up.

"Daddy won't you take me back to Muhlenberg County." No one could get that John Prine song out of their heads. But they heard many other sweet sounds. Tiffany Cook, a story subject putting her life back together at the Job Corps Center in Central City, sang out the line that sums up this brave, complicated, open-hearted place. "You show me you want success as bad as I do, and I'll help you." Amen.

• *Tom O'Neill*
National Geographic magazine

PHOTOS BY: TOP ROW, FROM LEFT, J. MARK KEGANS, KATHLEEN COLE, STUART BAUER, THOMAS CORDY
SECOND ROW: KATHLEEN FLYNN, CORY MITCHELL, PAUL CONRAD, JONATHAN KIRSHNER
THIRD ROW: J. MARK KEGANS, JUDI PARKS, KYUNG SOOK SCHOENMAN, JUDI PARKS
BOTTOM ROW: MARK ANDREWS, KYUNG SOOK SCHOENMAN, LISA KRANTZ, DANIEL WALLACE

THE MOUNTAIN WORKSHOPS | 3

Where paradise lay

traveling down the road

MUHLENBERG COUNTY, KENTUCKY

AT LEFT
• With lunch on his mind, Thomas Noffsinger starts his 1964 Cadillac DeVille and heads up Broad Street in downtown Central City.

AT RIGHT
• Sunrise pierces the stillness of a Mulhenburg County dawn.

BOTH PHOTOS
BY CHAD STEVENS

WORKSHOPS | 5

Where Paradise Lay | the faith in community

ABOVE • Jasmine Wells jokes with her grandfather, Willis Wells, in their living room on a weekend morning.

MUHLENBERG COUNTY, KENTUCKY

PHOTO BY SHAWN THEW

ABOVE • No one in the Whitehouse family – and there are 12 of them – eats until the prayer is over. From left are J.T., 13; Weston, 3; Jordan, 14; and Katie, 7. Their home is in Bremen.

PHOTO BY SARAH REINGEWIRTZ

Where Paradise Lay | friendship and fellowship

AT RIGHT • Rodney Kirtley, center, doesn't like being called "Judge." Nonetheless, he is the judge/executive of Muhlenberg County and oversees all financial and daily operations of the county. During a Lions Club luncheon, he shares a laugh with Lee Green and Dr. John Soderling.

PHOTO BY LAWRENCE JACKSON

ABOVE • Nelson the cat is the latest in a long line of pets in the Luther Ross family.

PHOTO BY MARK WEBER

MUHLENBERG COUNTY, KENTUCKY

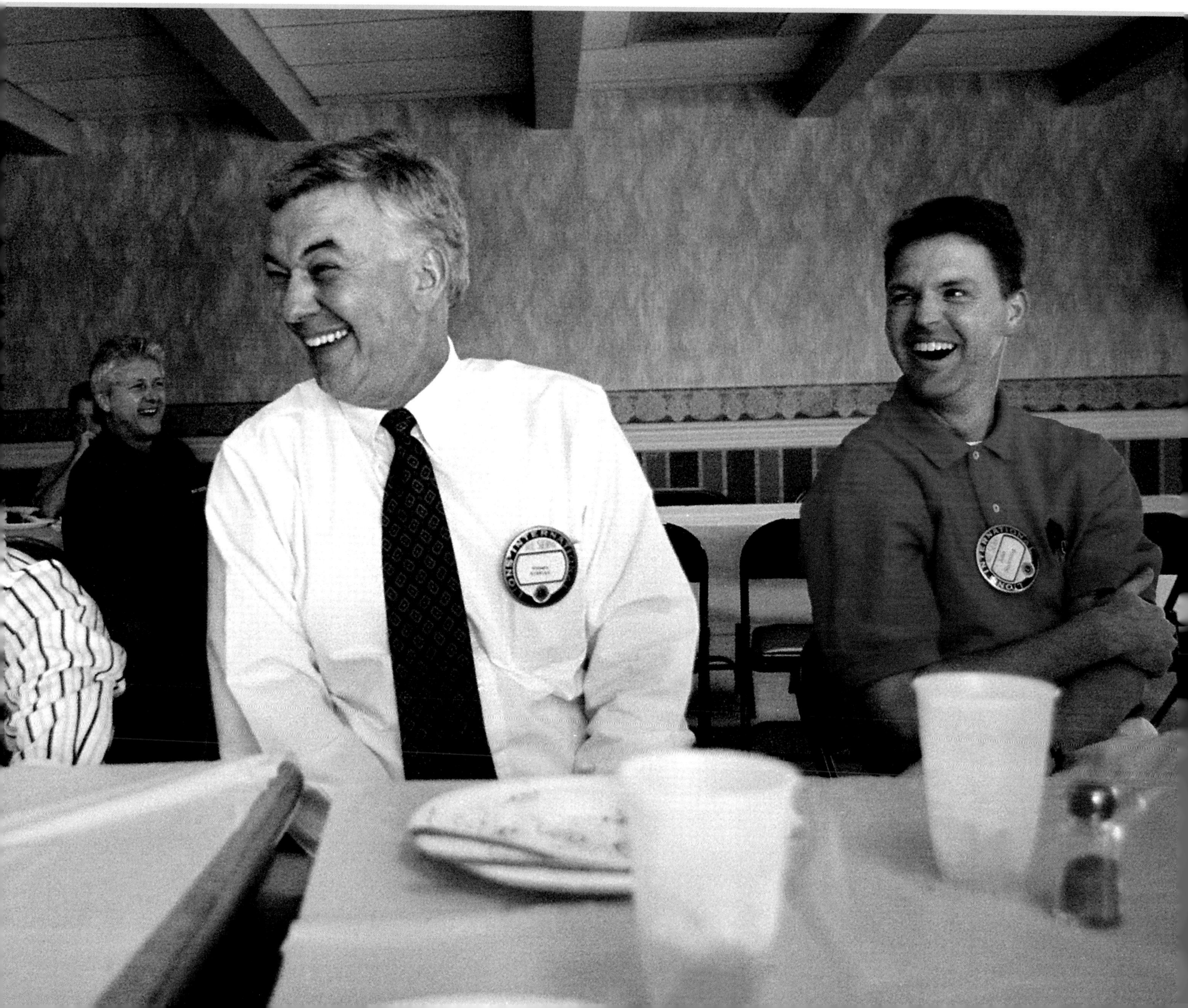

Where Paradise Lay | the long and the short of it

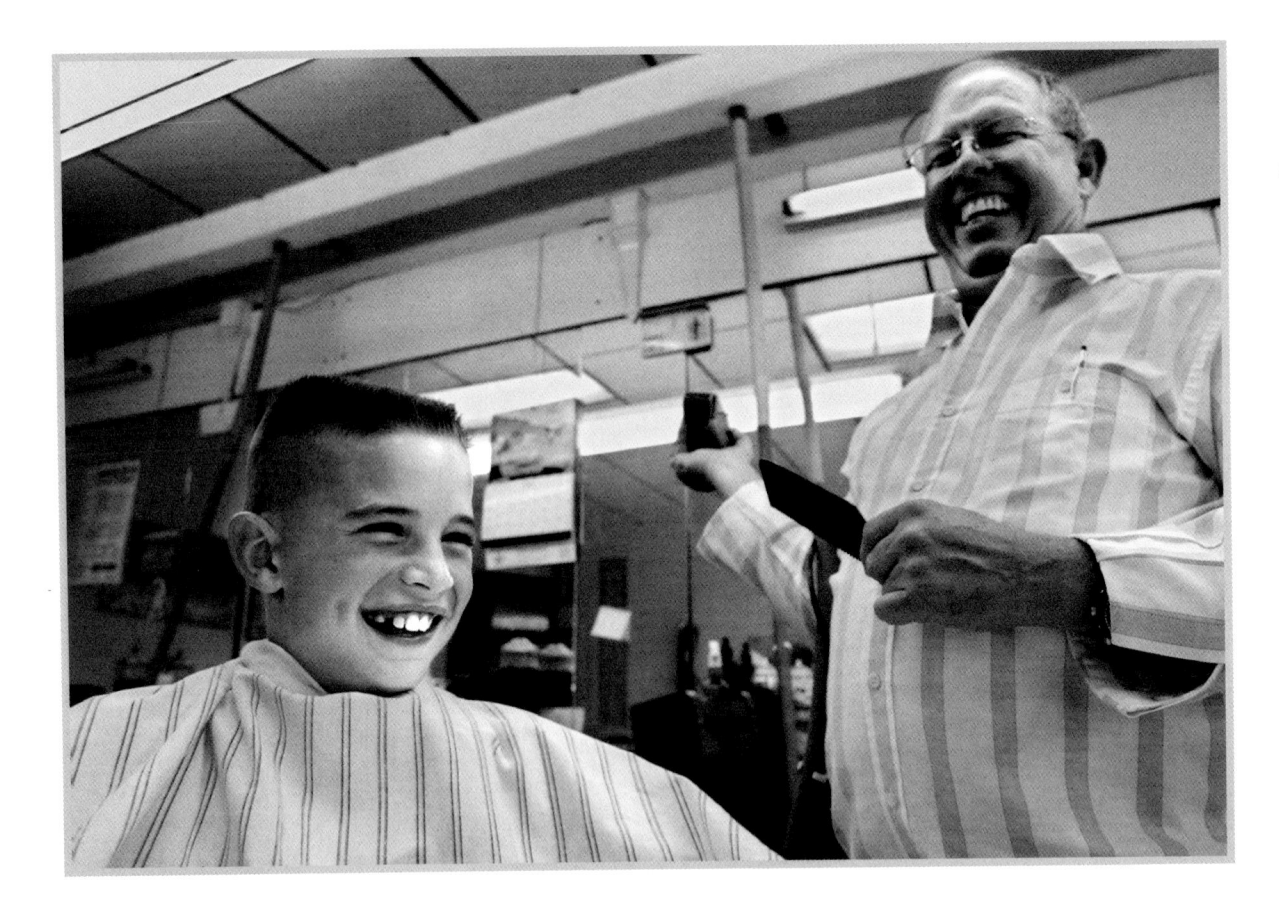

AT LEFT • Long-time barber Neville Ellison teases Vince Burns, 10, as he tells him that he's going to put "monkey pee" (hair tonic) on his hair so that all the girls will kiss him.

PHOTO BY AMBER WOOLFOLK

AT RIGHT • Jordan Whitehouse, 14, measures her 12-year-old sister Devan's hair at 32 inches. The girls' parents have never cut their hair because a Bible verse in Corinthians says it is glorious for a woman to have long hair and that it is given as covering. Devan measured Jordan's hair at 38 inches.

PHOTO BY SARAH REINGEWIRTZ

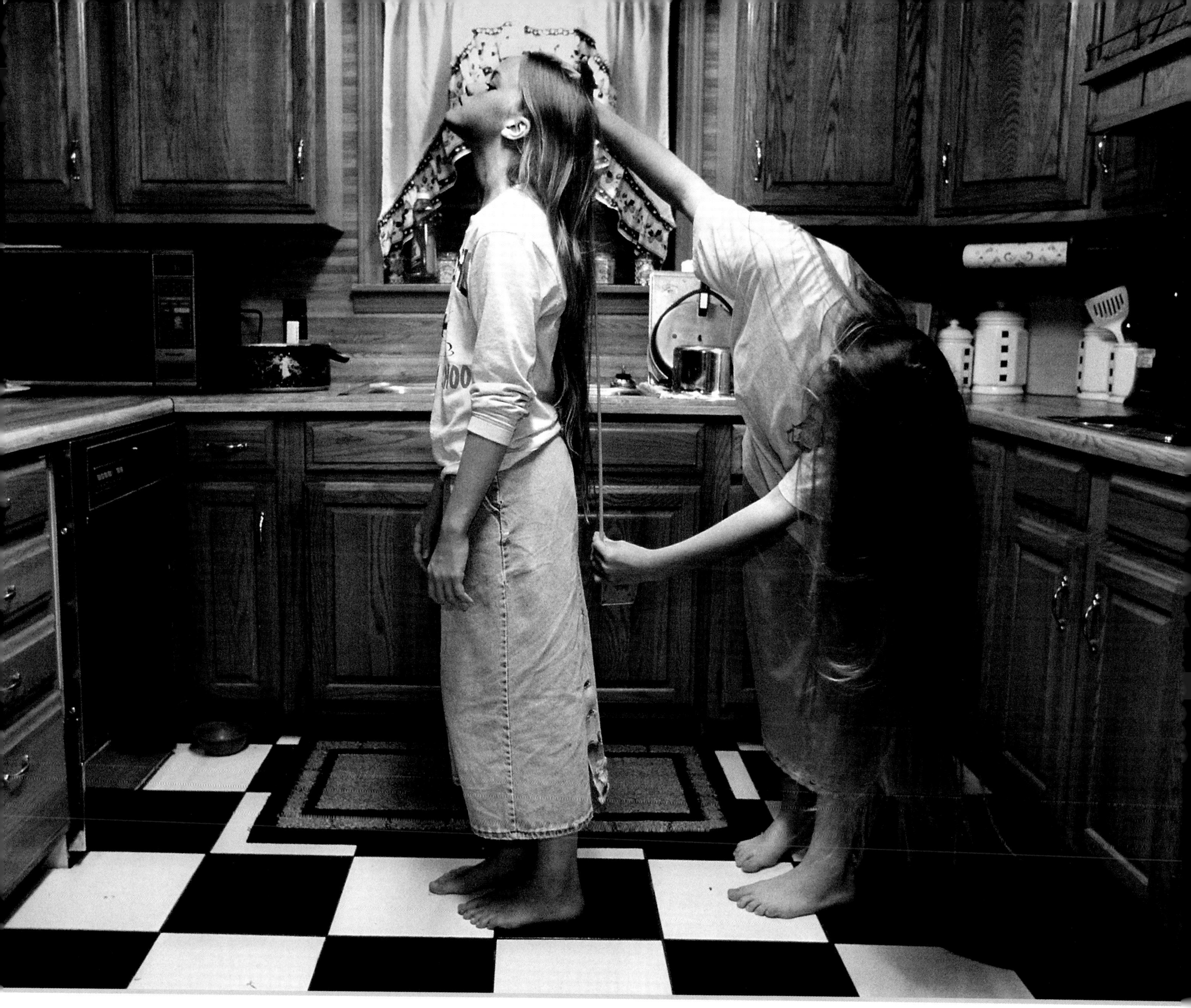

Where Paradise Lay | going our own ways

AT LEFT • Dorothy Swain is among the ladies who have their hair done at Carriage House Salon in Central City. "After you cut someone's hair for so long they become part of your family," says Davida Dukes, who runs the small salon in one of the town's oldest buildings.

PHOTO BY MARK HEDENGREN

AT RIGHT • Richard Sparks, 68, a resident of nearby Bremen, prays in his personal church of one. Designed in faith, the dripping red trim on the walls represents the blood of Christ.

PHOTO BY DAWN MAJORS

12 | MUHLENBERG COUNTY, KENTUCKY

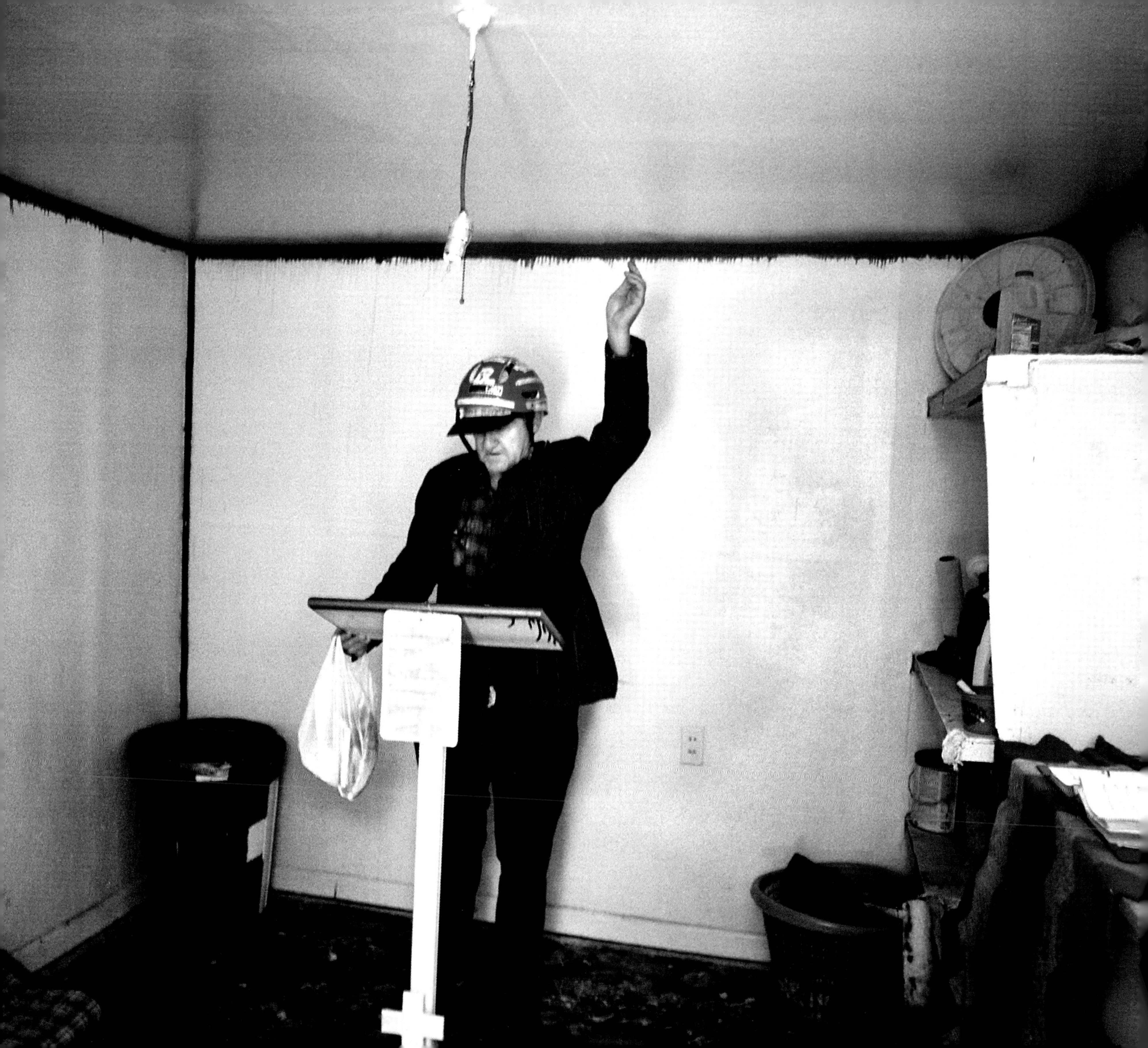

Where Paradise Lay | reaching for attention

ABOVE • Richard Spears has adopted many stray cats, which he cares for like they were his family. "I'm happy, satisfied and content all the time. I live a wonderful life."

MUHLENBERG COUNTY, KENTUCKY

PHOTO BY DAWN MAJORS

ABOVE • At the Any Image Tattoo Studio in Central City, 2-year-old Candace Travis, the daughter of owner Glenn Travis, seeks attention from her mother, Crystal.

PHOTO BY CHAD STEVENS

Where Paradise Lay | the stories of our lives

ABOVE • Edith Myers tells a story to Mary Singleton, a regular customer and friend. Mary visits the Uptown Cafe, where Edith is the cook, every day.

PHOTO BY MIRANDA ELLIS

MUHLENBERG COUNTY, KENTUCKY

ABOVE • "In the morning, my knuckles are stiff. I have to practice to warm them up," says 64-year-old thumb picker Royce Morgan.

PHOTO BY STEVE BUYANSKY

AT RIGHT • Julie Stewart tries to quiet her 15-year-old Chihuahua, Ditto, while he gets his yearly inoculation.

PHOTO BY JUDI PARKS

Where Paradise Lay

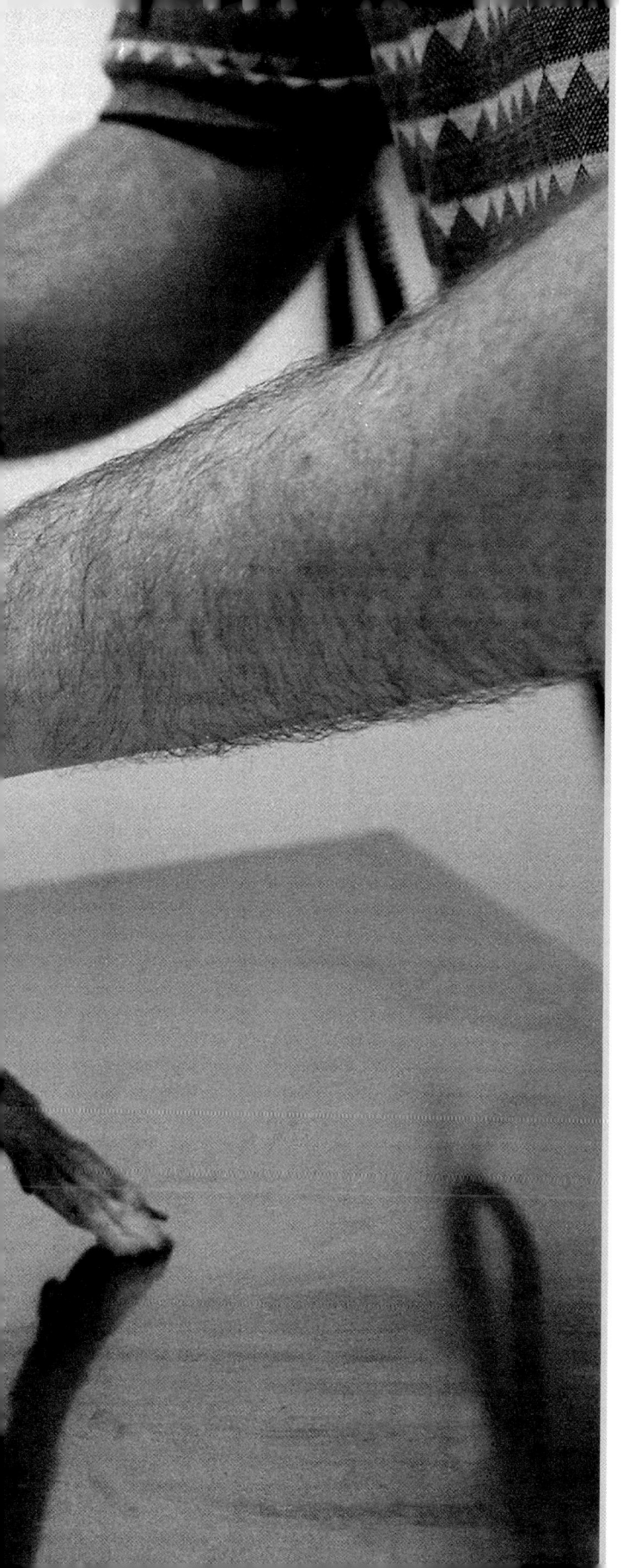

caring for our beloved

ABOVE • After work every day, Wendy Cessna visits her grandmother, Milbra Johnson, in the hospital. Since childhood, Wendy has been close to her grandmother, who now suffers from Alzheimer's disease.

PHOTO BY KYUNG SOOK SCHOENMAN

THE MOUNTAIN WORKSHOPS | 19

Where Paradise Lay | *just sitting around*

MUHLENBERG COUNTY, KENTUCKY

AT LEFT •
Wanda Steele clips her husband Texal's toenails on their front porch in Graham. "I don't mind doing it," she says. He worked in underground coal mines for 38 years and contracted black lung disease, which makes it difficult for him to do some things for himself.

AT RIGHT • An abandoned chair overlooks the banks of the Green River.

BOTH PHOTOS BY JONATHAN KIRSHNER

Where Paradise Lay | the King abounds

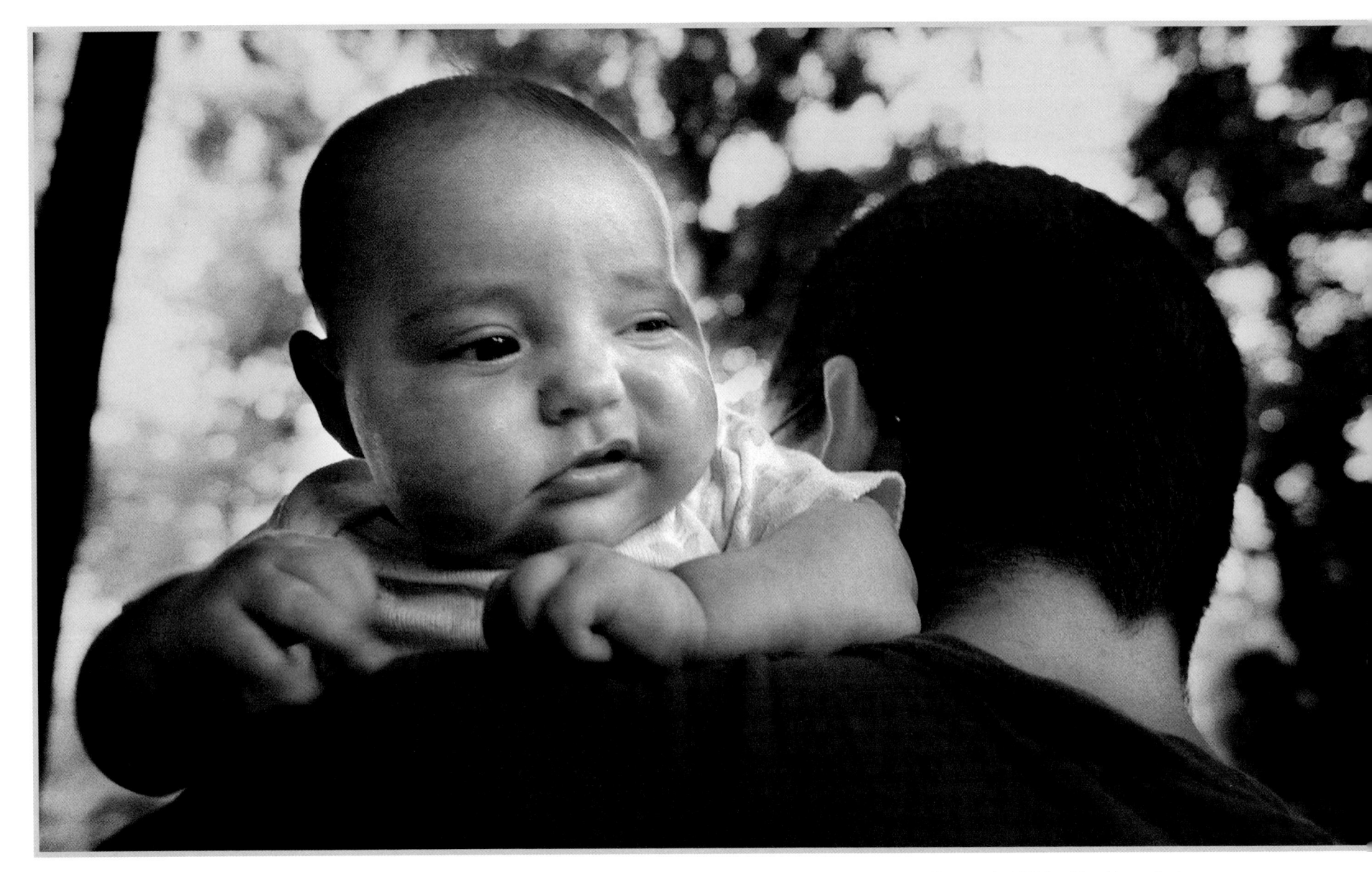

ABOVE • Five-month-old Haley Girard burps for her daddy, Mario Girard.

PHOTO BY LARRY POWELL

AT LEFT • Two-year-old Candace Travis peeks past a mural of Elvis painted on the window of Any Image Tattooing Studio in downtown Central City.

PHOTO BY KATHERINE GANTER

Where Paradise Lay

An introduction from Workshop Director Mike Morse

FACING PAGE • A slurry of burned coal is left behind the Tennessee Valley Authority's Paradise Power Plant.

PHOTO BY STUART BAUER

ABOVE • Shooter Mark Webber, photo coach Janet Reeves, shooter Lisa Krantz, editing students Rissa Miller and Ron Garrison discuss a photo edit of one of the stories shot during the week in Muhlenberg County.

PHOTO BY ROBIN BUCKSON

THE MOUNTAIN WORKSHOPS

began in 1976 with a field trip by the faculty and students of the newly formed photojournalism program at Western Kentucky University in Bowling Green. David Sutherland and I led the students' effort to document the last 11 one-room schoolhouses in Kentucky and Tennessee. It was a chance to do live photojournalism with people from an unfamiliar, vanishing culture.

Jack Corn joined Western's faculty in 1977 and conducted the Main Street Project, in which a group of Western photojournalism students documented a low-income area of Bowling Green and produced an audio-visual show. The next year, the workshop became more formal, with photo editors from area newspapers volunteering their time and expertise to coach participants at a workshop at Land Between the Lakes.

As the workshop evolved, working professionals began to participate, shooting side by side with students. The workshop grew steadily. More participants resulted in a need for more faculty, equipment and industry support. In 1997, the John S. and James L. Knight Foundation gave the photojournalism program a grant to purchase equipment so a picture editing division could be added.

The workshops' faculty and staff are among the top visual journalists in the world. This year, 50 shooters and 10 picture editors participated in the workshop. They were guided by 14 picture editing and shooting coaches; a professional support staff of 20 multimedia, sound, and writing professionals; several manufacturers' representatives; and a student-assistant crew of more than 20. In all, 115 students and professionals came together to share experiences, ideas, skills and understanding of what the profession can be at its best.

The workshop process is simple. We go to a rural town in south-central Kentucky or north-central Tennessee, set up a sophisticated network of digital equipment, and document the lives and culture of a cross-section of residents.

The purpose of the five-day visit is to get to know the residents and produce a book and a web site about them. Students, teamed with shooting, editing and writing coaches, expand their storytelling abilities by exploring the lives of their subjects.

The workshop is a 22-year labor of love on the part of the WKU faculty and an all-volunteer army of professional journalists with a passion for the profession and a willingness to give back to it. More than 200 of the world's best visual reporters, editors and managers have offered their expertise to more than 1,000 members of the visual journalism community.

Technological change is transforming our industry, but this workshop remains committed to documentary photojournalism education and the best ways of bringing the stories and lives of our subjects to light, whether it be through the printed page or new media.

ON THE FOLLOWING 70 PAGES ARE THE 26 PICTURE STORIES CHOSEN FOR DISPLAY IN THIS YEAR'S WORKSHOP BOOK.

PROMISES KEPT
Thomas Cordy, Jill Cretsinger
PAGES 26-29

A FRESH START
Seshu Badrinath, John Ballance
PAGES 30-31

ONE OF THE GUYS
Jonathan Kirshner, Jose Lopez
PAGES 32-33

EVERYBODY KNOWS CECIL
Paul Conrad, John Ballance
PAGES 34-35

CENTRAL CITY FIRE DEPARTMENT
George Callender, Linda Salazar
PAGES 36-37

A WILL TO WALK
Ethan Hyman, Susan F.B. Ryan
PAGES 38-41

THE OLD WOMAN IN THE SHOE
J. Mark Kegans, Jose R. Lopez
PAGES 42-45

BAKER'S DOZEN
Shayna Breslin, Amy Deputy
PAGES 46-49

KILROY
Shawn Thew, Stacy Hayes
PAGES 50-51

A TENDER TOUCH
Lawrence Jackson, Nerissa Miller
PAGES 52-53

FINDING A PLACE
Suzanne Feliciano, Jill Cretsinger
PAGES 54-55

A DYING DOWNTOWN
Chad Stevens, Caroline E. Couig
PAGES 56-59

A GIRL'S BEST FRIEND
Jill Snyder, John Ballance
PAGES 60-61

WORKING TOWARD HOME
Scott Andrews, Amy Deputy
PAGES 62-65

FAMILY MAN
Kathleen Flynn, Jill Cretsinger
PAGES 66-67

MORE THAN THE MAIL
Jaclyn McCabe, John Ballance
PAGES 68-69

'SPOON'
Kathleen Cole, Caroline E. Couig
PAGES 70-71

STARTING OVER
Katherine Ganger, Susan F.B. Ryan
PAGES 72-75

THE PICKIN' PLACE
Mark Weber, Ron Garrison
PAGES 76-77

CAN I GET A WITNESS?
Molly Van Wagner, Ron Garrison
PAGES 78-79

ROCK OF THE SPIRITUAL COMMUNITY
Alan Hale, Jill Cretsinger
PAGES 80-81

FLYING SOLO...
Michael Bunch, Linda Salazar
PAGES 82-83

WITH A LITTLE HELP...
Justin Rumbach, Caroline E. Couig
PAGES 84-87

CLOSING TIME...
Cara VanLeuven, Stacy Hayes
PAGES 88-91

FRIDAY NIGHT HERO
Neal Cardin & Linda Salazar
PAGES 92-93

BIRTH OF A NEW DAD
Tom Leininger, Kathy Wilcutt Cowan
PAGES 94-95

THE MOUNTAIN WORKSHOPS

I'll be good to you

Photography by THOMAS CORDY
Editing by JILL CRETSINGER

PROMISES, promises, promises. Elbert Fortney, 93, is a man who keeps his promises, says his wife, Lorene, 80.

"I'll be good to you," he told her three times before they married seven years ago.

"He's kept his promise," says Lorene.

A good example: Two weeks before their wedding, Elbert learned he would have to give half of his life savings to his children upon remarrying. He chose Lorene over the money. And she is just as caring.

"I get more kisses in a few days than I did in the last five years of marriage (to my first wife)," he says.

"My first wife was a Leo – see, that's a fire sign," Elbert says. "I'm a Scorpio, a water sign. You know what happens when fire and water mix, why they go ka-pssss. Now, we're both Scorpios – both water signs – and we're just flowing along."

"I don't know about them signs," Lorene says, "but I know that when two people have love ... things will work out. I don't know how to define it, but they just do."

On Tuesdays and Thursdays, the Fortneys visit the Muhlenberg County Senior Citizens Center, where they met.

Lorene started going to the center after her first husband died. Elbert noticed her during a card game there. A month later, Lorene said her phone started ringing. Seven months later they were married.

They still play rook and bingo at the center, where they gather with long-time friends.

"I like him because he's so easygoing," said Lorene. "You can't hold a man like him down."

ABOVE LEFT • Elbert and Lorene Fortney were married seven years ago. Elbert's first marriage lasted 66 years until his wife passed away. Lorene was married for almost 56 years before her first husband died.

ABOVE • Elbert and Lorene get a ride from her sister to the Kroger grocery store once a month. If the Fortneys forget anything, their neighbor brings the goods to them.

FACING PAGE • Lorene Fortney, 80, sweeps the back porch as Elbert, 93, returns from the barn.

MUHLENBERG COUNTY, KENTUCKY

THE MOUNTAIN WORKSHOPS | 27

I'll be good to you | continued...

"I know that **when two people have love**, things will work out. I don't know how to define it, but they just do."

•

Lorene Fortney

AT LEFT • The water level is down this year, and Elbert Fortney had to move their barbed wire fence to keep the horses out of the pond. Elbert keeps catfish in the pond and feeds them every morning.

AT RIGHT • The Pennyrile Allied Community Services shuttle bus takes the Fortneys to the Muhlenberg County Senior Citizens' Center. The fare is the service, which also serves the center for the mentally challenged, is a $1 donation.

28 | MUHLENBERG COUNTY, KENTUCKY

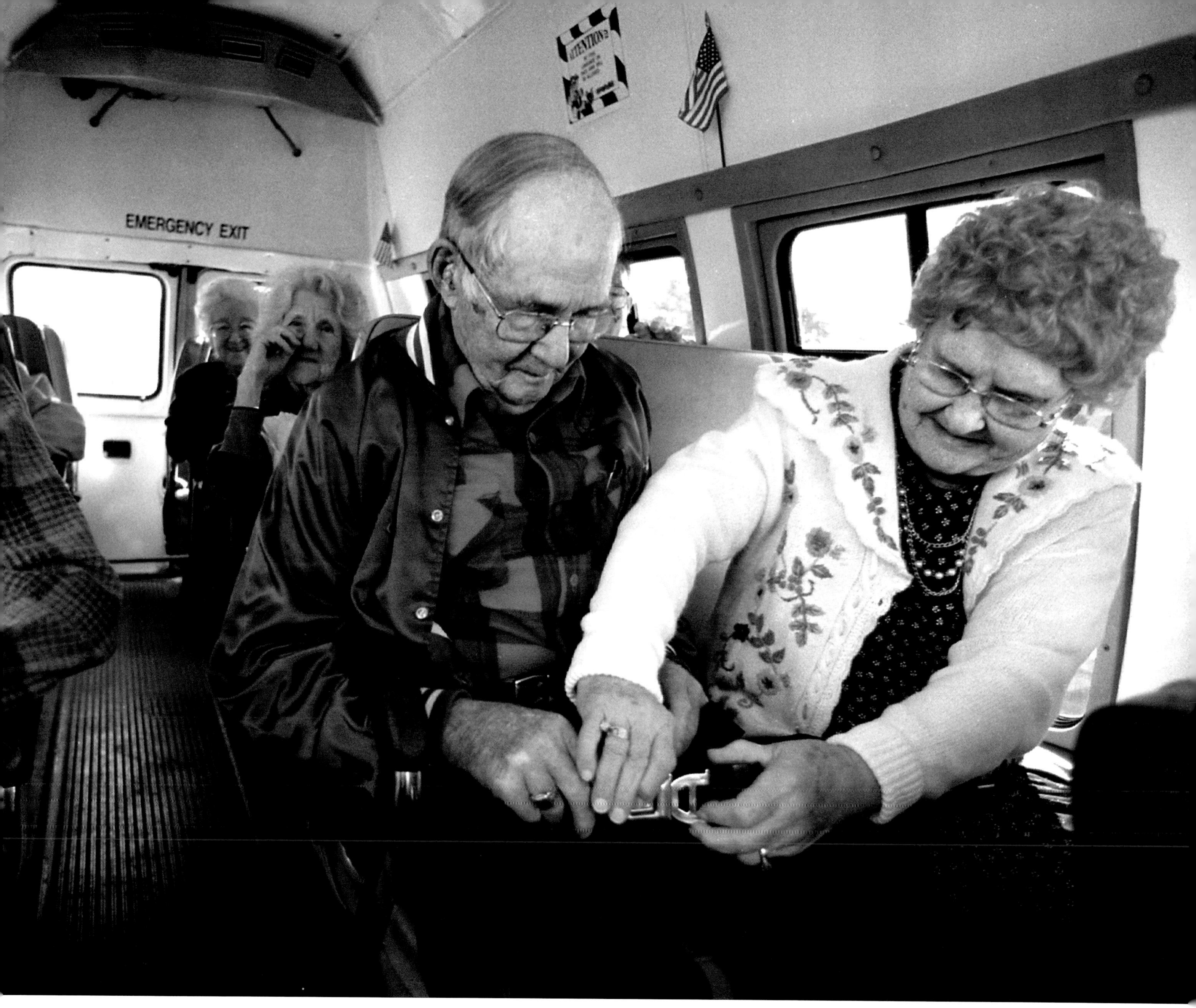
EMERGENCY EXIT

A fresh start

Photography by SESHU BADRINATH
Editing by JOHN BALLANCE

ABOVE • Shawn Kyncy guides her younger son, Cody, as he practices riding his bike without training wheels. She laments that her ex-boyfriend isn't around to share such moments with Cody and his other son, Casey. But she hopes the boys will remember that she was there when they needed her.

MUHLENBERG COUNTY, KENTUCKY

SHAWN

Kyncy's life is a juggling act. The single mother of two sons has gotten herself off welfare and found a job. Within five years she hopes to own a home and see Casey, 6, playing baseball and Cody, 4, pursuing a career in music.

Kyncy grew up in Indiana and lived in Tennessee and Arkansas with her sons' father before they broke up. She moved to Greenville at the suggestion of a friend. "It's better than being still with him," she says, then smiles. "The only fighting they hear now is me and them, just me and them."

Life can be hectic. "I am proud to raise my kids," she says. "They aren't doing without. They get food. They get toys. They get treats. They get clothing. They get love."

After the boys have been bathed and put to bed, Kyncy catches her breath and plans the future. She flips through a Fingerhut catalog, looking at things she can't afford now but would like to have someday. Her immediate goal is to replace her trusty but rusty Ford Tempo with a new-car. Not a brand-new car, she explains, but one that at least smells new.

"That new car smell," she says as she dreams. "I want that smell. Isn't that something, to want just a smell?"

ABOVE • Shawn Kyncy and her sons, Casey and Cody, wash the family car. The Ford Tempo has served them well, but Kyncy hopes to buy a newer model.

AT LEFT • Although Shawn Kyncy's time for herself is limited, she occasionally manages to visit with neighbors, play cards or go out in Madisonville.

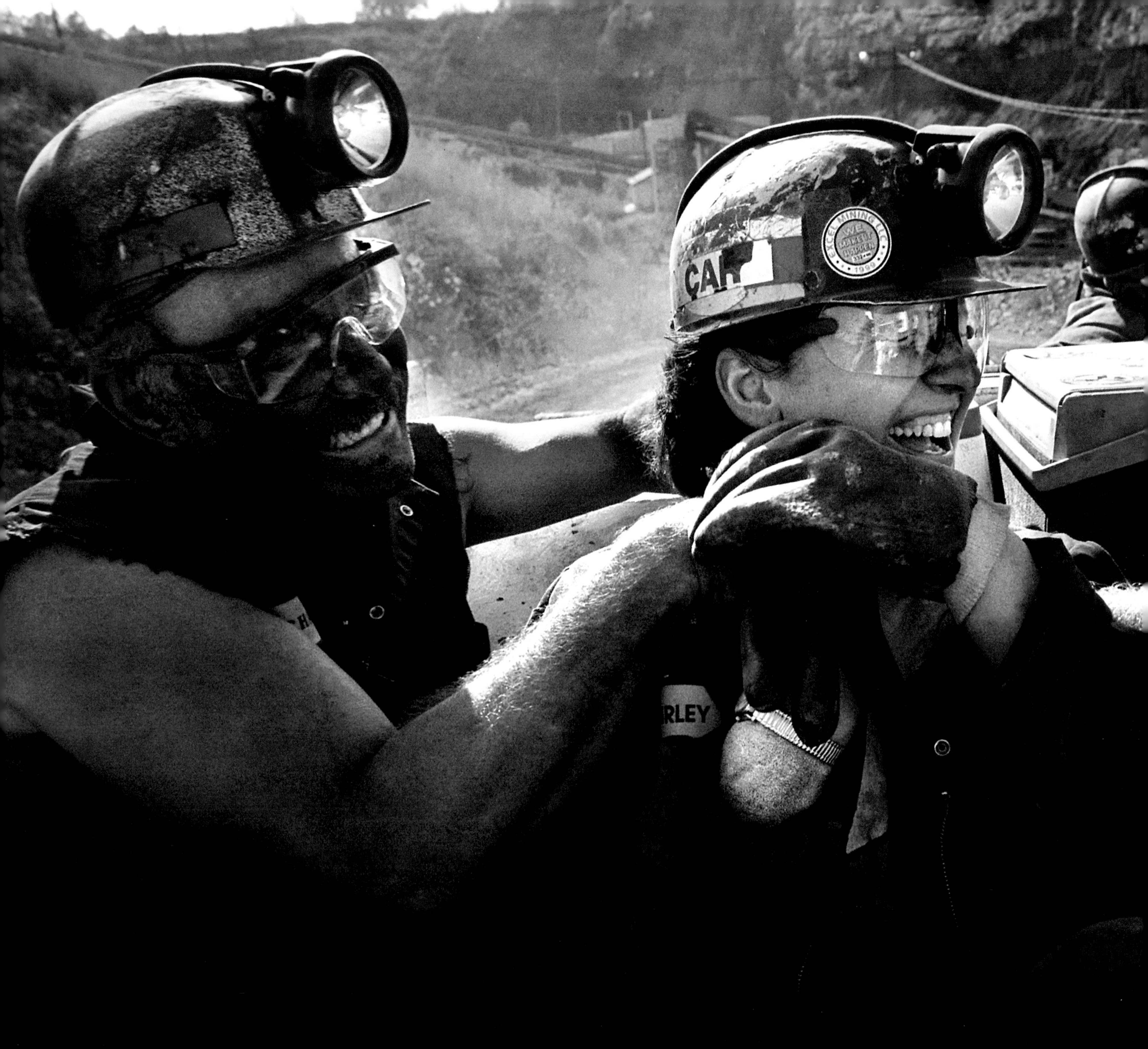
CAR
EXCEL MINING LLC
WE MAKE IT HAPPEN
1999
RLEY

She's one of the guys

Photography by
JONATHAN KIRSHNER
Editing by
JOSE R. LOPEZ

WITHIN the lightless chambers, the sweet voice of Shirley McLemore fights to be heard over the roar of machinery.

"I'll ring my bell and sing to them and tell them I love them just to pass the time and make people enjoy work," she says.

She is a coal miner and a coal miner's daughter who has learned to fight the harsh realities of working in a mine with laughter and song.

"All of us grew up like a bunch of boys, wrestling and all that," she says. Shirley has worked at Paradise #9 Mine near Central City since it opened in 1995. She met her husband of seven years, Alan, in the mines.

Life as a miner is dangerous. Her dad and stepdad were disabled from the mines.

"You question it a lot of times," Shirley says. "Have you made the right decision? I prayed before I went into the mines. Lord, you know I don't want to die in these mines. I don't believe anything serious will happen to me."

Light from the above-ground world begins to illuminate her dust-covered face. She begins to smile, emerging slowly from the dark below.

"A smile is one of the only things I know of that you can give away and always get it back," Shirley says.

FACING PAGE
• Richard Baize, left, and Ben Williams, put a wrestling hold on Shirley McLemore as they exit the Paradise #9 Mine at the end of their shift. "It never offends me if they say I'm one of the guys," Shirley says.

ABOVE • Though Shirley doesn't mind being known as one of the guys, she needs a separate dressing room at the end of her work shift.

Everybody knows Cecil

Photography by PAUL CONRAD
Editing by JOHN BALLANCE & NERISSA MILLER

AT RIGHT • Cecil Bard stops by Greenville's parks several times a day to give miniature badges to kids and talk to them about the role of a police officer. "It's good PR," he says.

BELOW • Cecil leaves the office after a slow but tiring day.

PATROLMAN Cecil Bard leans back in his chair, rubs his face and gives a heavy sigh. "Looks like it's going to be another slow day," he says, fidgeting with the pens on his desk.

Cecil, 36, has been on Greenville's 11-member police force for less than four years. But he has deep roots in Muhlenberg County. Like members of his family for 150 years, Cecil was born and raised here.

He graduated from Drakesboro High School, and his interest in police work led him to part-time work with the Muhlenberg County Sheriff's Department. Then, after attending Eastern Kentucky University, he joined the Greenville Police Department.

Cecil spends his days patrolling in an immaculately clean squad car and walking around town. As he makes his rounds, he smiles, waves and stops to chat. Drivers honk their horns and wave as they pass him.

"You learn a lot about what people are doing when you walk around," he says. "It's one of the things I like about the job – the people."

On slow days, he stops by Muhlenberg County Hospital to check on things. He also likes to visit the jail, where his mother, Earlene Williams, is a cook. "My mom's my best friend, next to my wife, Deborah," he says.

Cecil seems to have a lot of friends in Greenville. Wherever he goes, people stop to talk about everything, from the weather to what's going on in their lives.

"When the people get your trust, they'll talk about things they couldn't tell their husbands or wives," he says.

MUHLENBERG COUNTY, KENTUCKY

ABOVE • Greenville patrolman Cecil Bard adjusts his vest during a quick stop by his house one morning. A graduate of the Law Enforcement Academy at Eastern Kentucky University in Richmond, he received a citation for being Muhlenberg County's first African-American law enforcement officer. "A lot of people don't realize what the accomplishment is," Cecil says. "But it doesn't matter to me."

Central City Fire Department

Photography by GEORGE CALLENDER
Editing by LINDA SALAZAR

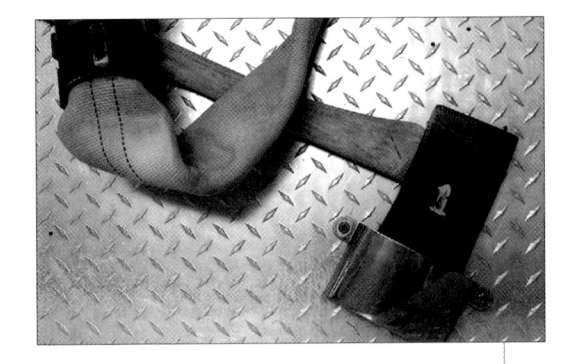

ABOVE • Tools of the trade at Central City Fire Department.

AT RIGHT • Firefighters roll a clothes dryer outside after it caught fire in a house across the street from the station.

BELOW • During a quiet night at the station the bay doors stay open.

JIMMY Moore and his son, Jimmy II, work there.
Jimmy's wife, Trudy, also helps out from time to time. Melissa House met her husband, Norman, there.

The place is the Central City Fire Department. And if you're looking for your cousin, uncle, brother, husband or wife, you'll likely find them at the station on North Second Street next to City Hall.

Most of the people you'll find at the station house are volunteer firefighters. They go there even when they are not responding to a call.

The department is composed of 45 volunteers, including two women, and eight firefighters paid by the city. The firefighters paid by the city also work as volunteers in their free time.

When the crew responded to a clothes dryer on fire one night in October, Trudy, the wife of Deputy Chief Moore, came in to answer phones in the dispatch booth. She brought her 5-year-old niece.

David LeGrand, assistant fire chief, says the firehouse is a good way to stay involved with the community. "You make new friends."

MUHLENBERG COUNTY, KENTUCKY

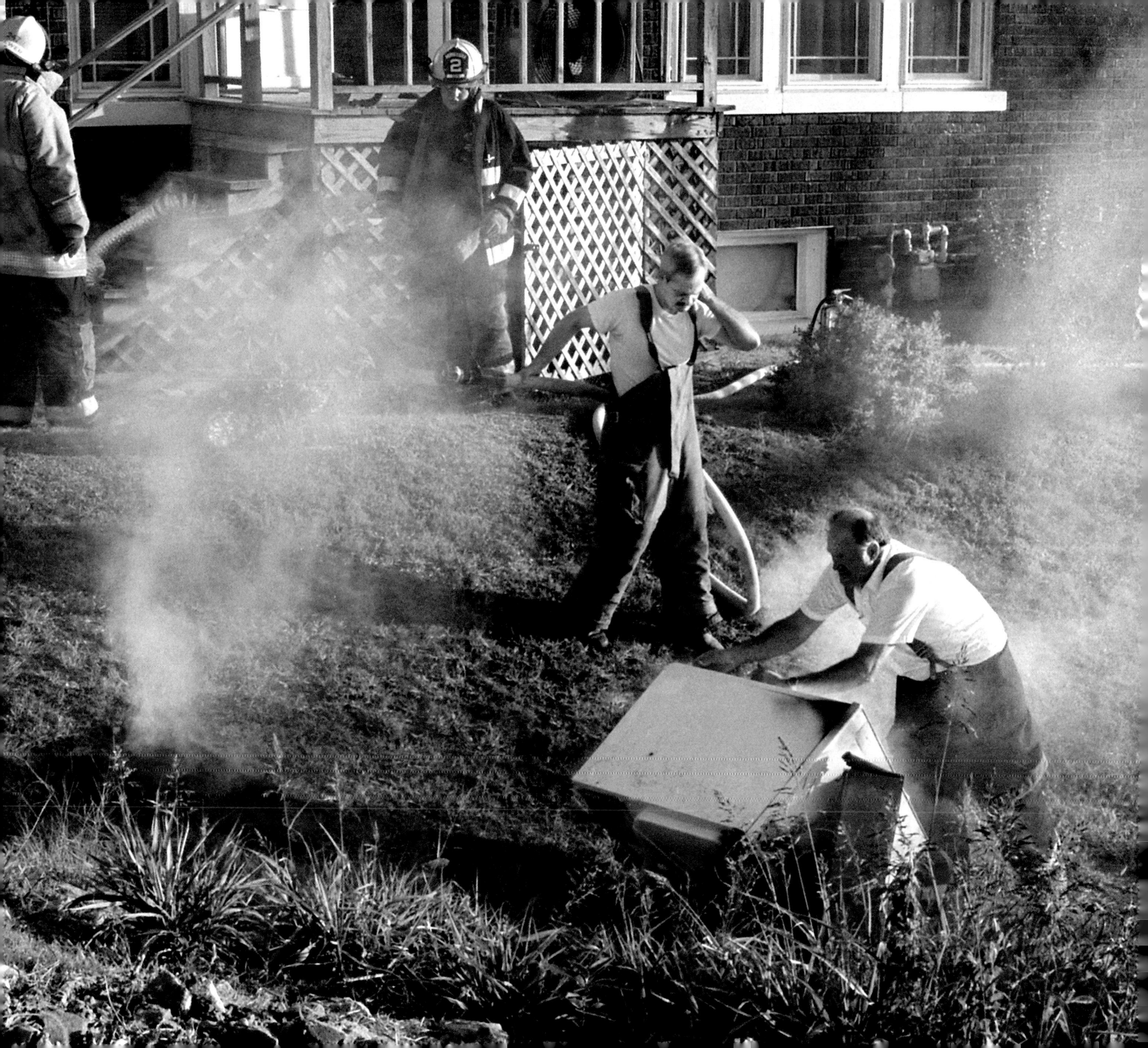

A will to walk

Photography by ETHAN HYMAN
Editing by SUSAN F.B. RYAN

THERE was a time when Chris Stinson could fly. He was a star basketball player for Hughes-Kirkpatrick High School, averaging 24 points a game. Now, at 32, he has multiple sclerosis, a degenerative disease that attacks the nervous system.

His speech is slurred; he cannot walk. "I need to keep a positive attitude because if you don't, it can get you quick," Chris says.

The first hint of the disease came when he was 18 and began suffering headaches and blurred vision. He was diagnosed with multiple sclerosis at 21.

When he was 26, Chris was engaged to be married. But the wedding fell through.

Now he lives with his mother, father, brother and grandmother in his parents' spacious new home in rural Dunmor. His mother, Judy, takes care of the house and devotes much of her life to him.

"If it wasn't for my mom, I would be in bad shape," Chris says. "She cooks, she washes my clothes, she does everything."

She gives him a daily shot of Copaxone, a drug that helps prevent the progression of multiple sclerosis. It's a painful ordeal. Chris cools down the area with ice until his skin turns white. Then he turns his head. He can't stand to watch.

"I dread it," Chris says.

The disease also has forced Chris to give up his greatest love, fishing. He owned a bass boat that could reach about 70 mph, but was forced to sell it after an attack several years ago.

"I would give anything for that bass boat back," he says, looking through a boating magazine.

In the meantime, the family prays for a cure. "I will probably have to go through this some more," Chris says, "but I know someday I will walk again."

ABOVE • Since he cannot stand up without a walker, Chris shaves while lying in bed.

FACING PAGE • Chris rests after getting his daily shot of Copaxane, a drug that helps prevent the progression of multiple sclerosis.

A will to walk | continued...

ABOVE • Before dinner, the family says grace. The Stinsons are active in the Hillcrest Church of Christ, and Chris attends whenever he feels strong enough.

AT RIGHT • Judy is always around for Chris. When not attending to him, she is constantly in motion, finding chores around the house. "Everywhere you look, there is work to do," she says.

40 | MUHLENBERG COUNTY, KENTUCKY

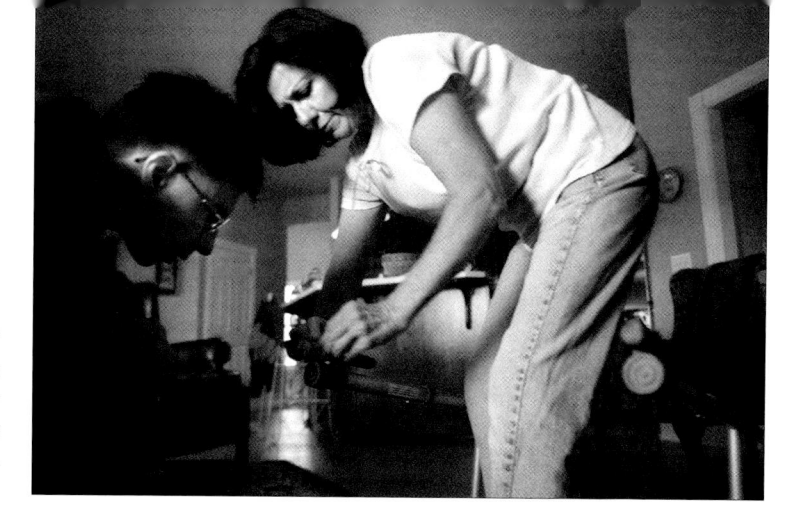

AT RIGHT • "I'm here if you need me," Judy tells Chris. She assists him in many ways, including helping him put leather pads around the brakes of his walker to keep them from scuffing the floors.

BELOW • Every day, Chris exercises in the family's indoor swimming pool, which they included for Chris when the house was built. The buoyancy of the water gives Chris the ability to walk; it gives him freedom he cannot get out of water.

The old woman in the shoe

Photography by J. MARK KEGANS
Editing by JOSE R. LOPEZ

JOAN Kindrick is the calm eye in a nine-hour storm of spilled milk and little hugs.

The maelstrom begins with the arrival of "her kids" every weekday morning at Kindrick's home day care on Paradise Street in Greenville.

To the parents of those kids, many of whom she cared for over 20 years ago, she is a saint. One friend says Joan is "The Old Woman in the Shoe."

Quick to deflect any compliments with modesty, Joan, who has three grown children of her own, says what she does just comes naturally to her.

"Kids have always been my life," she said. "Ever since I can remember, all I wanted to do was take care of babies."

Quick with a tickle, an "I love you" or a slice of "granny toast," "Joanie" is popular with the kids.

The bond between "Joanie" and the children is not lost on the parents.

"We took our kids to Disney World last week and they were more excited about returning to Joan's on Monday morning than they were the whole week in Florida," said Ruth Tarter, mother of Zachary and Elizabeth.

AT RIGHT • Two-year-old Lilly Tinsley is torn between her mother and Joan Kindrick as she begins another day under Joan's watchful eye.

ABOVE • Joanie's kids, from left to right: Lauren Sparks, Zachary Tarter, Ann Taylor Sparks, Elizabeth Tarter, Graham Sparks, Michael Higgs, Sydnie Driskill, Quinten Travis, Eli Travis, and Grant Ferguson.

AT LEFT • Elizabeth Tarter, 7, talks with "Miss Joanie," as the kids call her, at the day-care center one October morning.

THE MOUNTAIN WORKSHOPS | 43

The old woman in the shoe | continued...

AT LEFT
• Being outside means room to romp for Lilly Tinsley and Graham Sparks.

AT TOP RIGHT
• Zachary Tarter, 4, is the odd boy out in a card game between 7-year-olds Lauren Sparks and Elizabeth Tarter.

AT BOTTOM RIGHT • "I just go in circles trying to keep every kid happy," says Kindrick, as she serves lunch to the 11 children she cares for.

"I treat them **just like my own kids...** There is never a dull moment."

•

Joan "Miss Joanie" Kindrick

THE MOUNTAIN WORKSHOPS | 45

Baker's dozen

Photography by SHAYNA BRESLIN
Editing by AMY DEPUTY

MUHLENBERG COUNTY, KENTUCKY

THE DANIEL FAMILY

doesn't watch TV. They don't curse, drink or tell off-color jokes, go to the movies, buy magazines, play video games, use computers, or spend time at the mall.

Not one of the seven Daniel girls has ever had a single strand of her hair cut, never. Not one of the six Daniel family boys has ever worn a pair of shorts, never.

Tony and Debbie Daniel don't wear wedding rings. In fact, no one in the Daniel family wears a single piece of jewelry. When someone in the Daniel family gets sick they don't go to the family doctor. They have no family doctor. This family belongs to the Holiness Church, and they follow the teachings of the New Testament as literally and strictly as possible.

"I feel this is the way God wants me to live – by the Bible," Debbie says. "I feel this is the road for me. I don't feel there are sacrifices that's not got its rewards."

Forty-one-year-old Debbie Daniel delivered every single one of her 13 children at home, including 2 1/2-week-old David Kyle. Forty-year-old Tony Daniel has watched each one of his children born in the same house with only the help of midwives.

One birth was particularly difficult.

"My grandmother, Debbie's midwife, said, 'Debbie, if God don't move for you this time you'll die.'" It was a moment of truth. Tony was afraid, and ready to head for the hospital. Debbie chose to stay home and accept God's will, Tony says. She made it.

AT LEFT • "People call us a baker's dozen; we hear that a lot," Debbie Daniel says. The family includes, in front row, Jennifer Rachelle, 15; Teleah Jane, 20; Allison Dawn, 6; Tony Sr., 40; David Kyle, 2 1/2 weeks; Debbie, 41; Joseph Lane, 2; Deborah LeAnn, 12; Kristi Brooke, 14 and Bethany Renee, 4. In back are Timothy Lynn, 8; Stephanie Shea, 10, and Steven Wayne, 9. Two married children are not pictured.

AT LEFT • Each weekday morning Debbie and 10 of her children ride to the Holiness Church school. "They're not exposed to the drugs and stuff like public schools..." says their father.

BELOW • After school the Daniel kids burst out of the van, change into play clothes and run to the shed for their bikes.

THE MOUNTAIN WORKSHOPS

Baker's dozen continued...

ABOVE • When one little one gets going on a playful streak, the energy is contagious and often they will keep the entire family up late dancing, chasing, wrestling and teasing each other.

ABOVE • Parenting, "... It takes years of experience. You've got to be able to give a lot. If you are selfish, it doesn't work," Tony says.

ABOVE • When it's time for dinner Debbie and Tony have to plan just when to call the kids in. "As you can tell they don't get whoopin's near often enough," Tony says half-teasing.

ABOVE • Debbie explains what brings her the greatest joy, "Pleasing my children and Tony and bringing a newborn baby into the world – it's wonderful."

ABOVE • "It's real joyful to see how the kids react to a newborn when they get back home," Debbie says. "With the newborn baby everybody wants to help. They've been around babies all their life. There's just always been babies." Debbie trusts her infant to the care of her 10-year-old daughter Stephanie.

Kilroy

Photography by SHAWN THEW
Editing by STACY HAYES

At 5 a.m. every day, Leroy "Kilroy" Willis drives around Greenville checking banks before employees arrive. By 7:30 a.m. he has been home, eaten breakfast, changed into his deputy sheriff's uniform, and is on his way to a day as bailiff in the county courts

At 4 p.m. he exchanges his badge and gun for a broom and dustpan and walks across the street to his night job as a custodian at National Bank.

From Brothers' Bar-B-Que, to the court clerk's office, to the defendants' bench in district court, people say the same things about Kilroy: He always has time to say hello and chat. He is a man who will treat you fairly and with respect.

"He's a legend, really," Sheriff Jerry Mayhugh says.

ABOVE • Deputy sheriff Leroy "Kilroy" Willis heads back to the sheriff's office after chatting with friends at the post office. Kilroy is well known around the county. "I know everybody," he says. "I don't know if that's good or bad."

MUHLENBERG COUNTY, KENTUCKY

"When I think of retiring, I'm just afraid that I won't be satisfied."

• *Leroy "Kilroy" Willis*

ABOVE • Kilroy rests one Friday afternoon while his granddaughter, Jasmine Wells, talks with her cousin, Laura Owens. Normally, Kilroy would not have been home, but it was a school holiday and he was waiting for Jasmine's dad to pick her up.

AT LEFT • Kilroy watches over Brandy Eversol, front row, and other prisoners as they await trial in Muhlenberg County District Court.

THE MOUNTAIN WORKSHOPS

A tender touch

Photography by LAWRENCE JACKSON
Editing by NERISSA MILLER

DEBBIE Koonce's first visit of the day takes her to the home of Katherine and Elmer Noffsinger. She enters their home with the ease of a friend, but she's more than that – she's a registered nurse with Regional Medical Center Home Health.

The Noffsingers are in their '90s, and Elmer is recovering from pneumonia. He sits in the living room with his head held low, barely acknowledging her as she checks his vital signs. So she directs her questions to Katherine.

"Is he eating? How much? Good." Then Debbie goes through a list of instructions that Katherine must follow until her next visit. She goes over everything twice, and has Katherine repeat many of the instructions.

Her next stop is the home of Henry and Mae Vincent. Henry had surgery on his ankle the previous week, and Debbie must change his bandages. But she also asks about the Vincents' family, and gives Henry a hard time about his trying to do too much, too soon after surgery.

Then Debbie is back in her car, winding along the roads of Muhlenberg County on a crisp fall day.

"I love this time of the year," she says.

(Editor's note: Elmer Noffsinger, 91, died on March 28, 2000.)

ABOVE • Debbie Koonce, left, enjoys a light moment with Wendy Hardison, a lab technician at Muhlenberg Community Hospital, as she drops off a set samples to be tested.

AT RIGHT • "I love this time of year," says Debbie, a registered nurse who drives around Muhlenberg County to make house calls on those who cannot visit a doctor's office.

MUHLENBERG COUNTY...

ABOVE • Debbie waves goodbye to Henry Vincent and his wife, Mae, after going to their home to change bandages on Henry's ankle. Henry's ankle had been operated on a week earlier.

THE MOUNTAIN WORKSHOPS | 53

Finding a place

Photography by **SUZANNE FELICIANO**
Editing by **JILL CRETSINGER**

"I'M getting everything I ever wanted out of life," Tiffany Stoker says. But first she had to get what she needed.

Stoker quit school when she was 15 and ran away from an abusive father and a mother ill with colon cancer. She supported herself by baby-sitting and mowing lawns.

A brush with the Florida juvenile system at 16 brought Stoker to the Earle C. Clements Job Corps Center in Muhlenberg County. Authorities gave her a choice — go to the center or be returned to her parents.

Stoker realized she needed an education and a new, supportive environment.

"If it wasn't for Job Corps, I'd probably be in jail," says Stoker, 19. While at the Job Corps center, Stoker earned her GED and learned to operate heavy equipment, fix cars, do security work, shop, cook and live on her own. Now she is studying facilities maintenance.

Despite her rough start in life, Stoker was never in trouble at the center. "We feel like we've pretty much raised her," says Suzanne Thornton, the center's Student Government Association coordinator.

In November, Stoker and a friend plan to join the Navy. Stoker wants a career that will keep her physically active and put her around a lot of people. "Man, I'm gonna be tearing it up in boot camp."

AT LEFT • Tiffany Stoker says she is comfortable with who she is. "Sometimes I think she's older than I am," says acquaintance David Childress about the teen-ager with the pierced tongue and two-toned bleached-blond hair. Stoker and George Baldwin share a chair while watching a movie after a class.

ABOVE • Tiffany Stoker works on a lawn mower while fellow Job Corps student Christor take a break.

AT LEFT • Corey Churn gets a lift from Stoker as they horse around after a class in facilities management. She enjoys being different. Friends gave her the nickname "Freak Tigger" after the Winnie the Pooh character who boasts, "I'm the only one."

A dying downtown

Photography by CHAD STEVENS
Editing by CAROLINE E. COUIG

AT RIGHT • There isn't much for teen-agers to do in downtown Central City. Taylon Whitney, 13, had to stop riding his bike after he popped the rear tire on the curb.

BELOW • Downtown Central City's scarcity of customers has left James Allen Seaton, owner of Central City Loans, with a lot of time on his hands. "You have to be a nut to try to run this place," he said.

AS IT HAS in so many small communities across the country, competition from the chain stores has made downtown Central City a shadow of its former self.

Dozens of downtown merchants have called it quits: Buddy's Hardware, Cohen's Department Store, Barnes Mercantile, Miss Ida's Gift Shop, the M&R Shop. Between increased competition and the demise of the coal industry, none of them made it.

Brand's Corner Drugstore hung on for nine more years, but had to make some changes. No more toys, beauty products or school supplies. Just the pharmacy and favors – like the time Brand shuttled a roll of film to a customer who'd called him on Christmas Eve, frantic she wouldn't get pictures of the kids.

"You just have to go out of your way," recalled Brand, who retired and closed the doors in 1990. "I think that's what kept us going good."

Bill Greenwood was literally born into downtown life. His father established Barnes Mercantile, a retail fixture that lasted 44 years before it lost the battle.

"I grew up listening to the history of Broad Street – of what Central City used to be like," said Greenwood, president of the 100-year-old Lawton Insurance Agency. "When I saw it disappearing, I thought, 'I have to do something about this.'"

So on the lot where the family store once thrived, he's building what he hopes will be downtown's salvation – The Courtyard, an assisted-living housing complex with 38 apartments. He hopes the facility will bring the people, the people will bring the businesses, and the businesses will bring a new life to downtown.

"We have to look ahead," he added. "This might just end up being a great place to live."

ABOVE • For 55 years Sue Wheeldon has owned property downtown, but only one tenant remains in her apartment building on Broad Street. Wheeldon had worked for 15 years at the J.C. Penney store before it burned in 1964.

A dying downtown   continued...

ABOVE • Bill Whitmer's Broadway Jewelry has survived it all – the end of the railroad, the J.C. Penney fire, the demise of the coal industry and the arrival of the chain stores. Even after 51 years, he has no plans of retiring. "In fact, I'm going to wait until my 5-year-old grandson is old enough to take over," Whitmer said.

AT LEFT • With the last few minutes of his lunch break ticking away, Ferrell Christmas, part-owner of the Uptown Cafe, washes down the last bite of his "Ding-Dong" dessert with Arthur Waddell, left, and Christmas's wife, Mae, right, another part owner.

BELOW • Morning light stretches across Broad Street, the main artery of downtown Central City.

A girl's best friend

Photography by JILL SNYDER
Editing by JOHN BALLANCE

AT RIGHT • Laina Seay, who loves to draw and write, sketches in her room, which is filled with trophies and other horse memorabilia. Laina says owning a horse is fun, but also a lot of work.

BELOW • Ashley Dukes, left, Laina Seay, center, and Amanda Hunter are members of the Muhlenberg County Riding Rampage 4-H drill team. The team, coached by Laina's mother, Jan Watkins, has won the state championship five out of the past six years.

LAINA Seay's best friend is patient and trusting and never gives her a hard time. He is also more than 7 feet tall. "Me and King, we've been buddies forever," she says.

King, who has been Laina's horse for 10 years, is one of 13 horses on her family's farm. Laina has been around horses her whole life. Her mother, Jan Watkins, taught her to ride King when she was 3, just barely big enough to hold the reins. Now Laina performs with the Muhlenberg County Riding Rampage 4-H drill team and competes in barrel races.

Laina, 13, says a special bond develops between horse and rider. "It is a relationship built on trust," she says.

When Laina talks about King, she describes the characteristics of a good friend: he listens, he is patient, he is trusting and loyal. She puts her life in his hands every time she saddles up.

By having her own horse, Laina is living many young girls' dream. But she says there is another side to that dream.

"It's a lot of hard work and doesn't smell very good," Laina says. She helps feed the horses. She grooms them. And once a week, she shovels out their stalls.

But Laina doesn't mind doing a favor for a friend.

MUHLENBERG COUNTY, KENTUCKY

ABOVE • Three of the 13 horses on Laina Seay's family farm are Bud, left, King, rear, and Coty. Laina says horses sometimes can be better listeners than people.

Working toward home

Photography by SCOTT ANDREWS
Editing by AMY DEPUTY

AT RIGHT • Mariano holds a photo of his 6-month-old daughter.

BELOW • Pedro, right, and Ascension begin morning chores.

EVERY year for the past three years, Mariano Meza Duran has left Mexico to work in the tobacco and corn fields of L.E. Pearson's 1,200-acre farm.

At home, he can earn $30 a week.

In Kentucky, he earns $250 a week.

The money is good, but the separation from his family is not. Mariano leaves home in May and he doesn't return until December.

Mariano says his first child, a girl, was 6 weeks old when he left his home in Mexico. She is 6 months old now. Mariano says it pains him that he must be absent while she grows up.

He said he would bring his wife and child to live with him in America, but Kentucky law prohibits spouses and children of Mexican migrant workers from joining their families in America.

Ascension Hernandez and Pedro Gonzales are Mariano's roommates, workmates and constant companions. Their camaraderie and constant joking help lighten the burden of separation.

Often, when the joking lapses, their eyes become distant. In December, they will return to the pacific coast of Mexico, where their wives and families wait.

AT RIGHT • When they're not working, Mariano, Ascension and Pedro pass the time in their trailer. They seldom go to town so they can save money to send to their families.

MUHLENBERG COUNTY, KENTUCKY

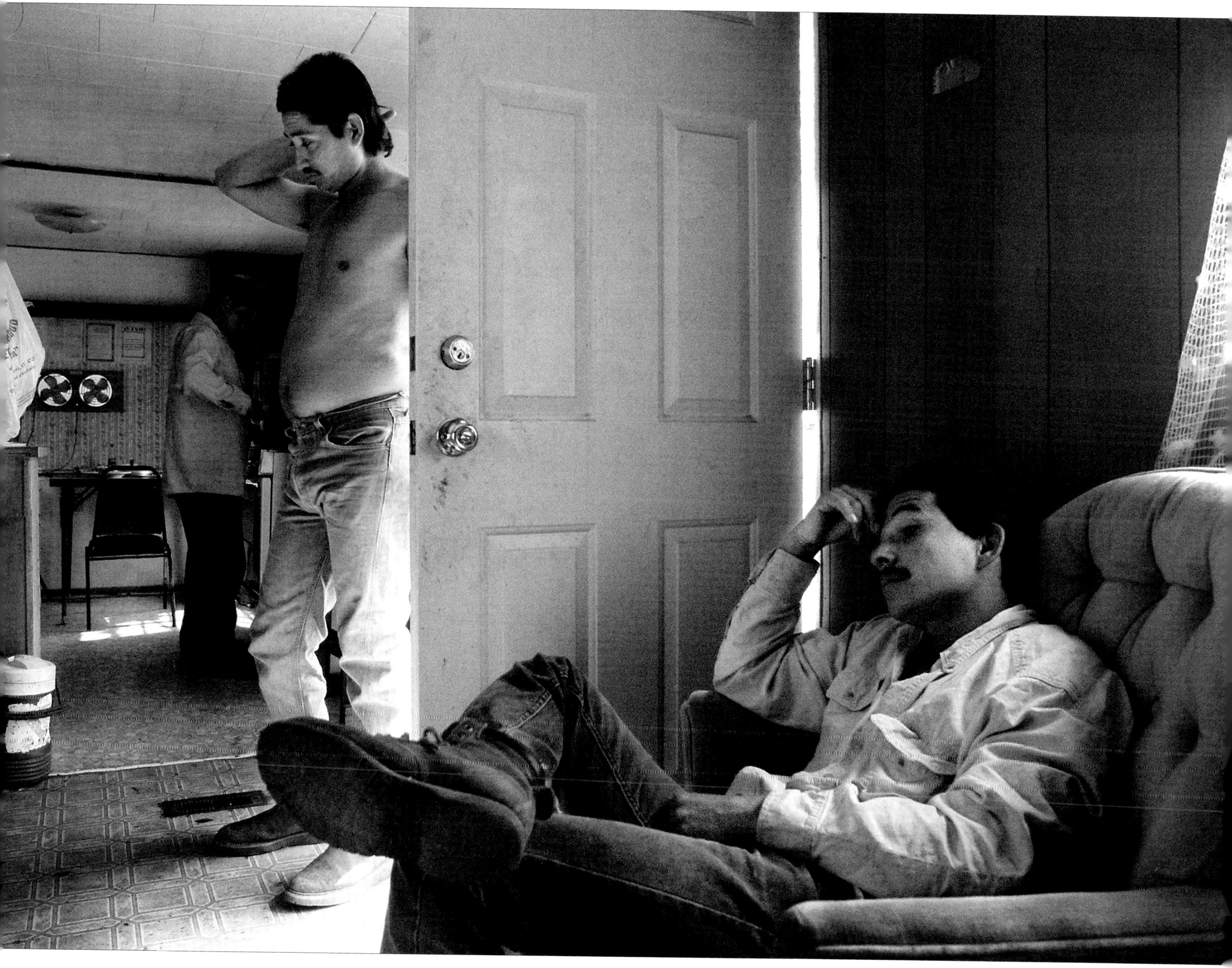

Working toward home | continued...

AT LEFT • Timmy Johnson jokes with Pedro and Mariano as they break for a cigarette. Timmy, 12, lives near the Pearson farm.

AT RIGHT • Pedro leaves the barn where tobacco is being "smoked" to add flavor.

AT LEFT • Pedro says he is fortunate to have a washing machine. But there is no dryer, so he hangs his work clothes on the clothesline behind the barn.

> " A campesino is **a farmer with no land — I am a campesino.**"
>
> •
>
> *Mariano Meza Duran*

64 | MUHLENBERG COUNTY, KENTUCKY

THE MOUNTAIN WORKSHOPS | 65

Family man

Photography by KATHLEEN FLYNN
Editing by JILL CRETSINGER

SINCE he graduated from high school 22 years ago, Gary Pierce has worked at Ensign Bickford Co.'s nitration plant in Graham. As the senior control room technician, he oversees the production of nitric acid and acetone used in explosives.

"We really have to trust each other here," he says. "We're like a family."

The plant was built to support the local mining industry. "At one time Muhlenberg County was the leading coal producer in the world," Pierce says. "Not anymore. When I graduated from high school, all of my friends worked in the mines. Now none of them do."

Pierce takes pride in his work. He hasn't missed a day in five years, and he has been rewarded for ideas that improved the plant. When he's not checking gauges and making sure things are running smoothly, he passes time reading the newspaper, dipping tobacco and spinning in his chair.

The highlights of Pierce's week are Tuesday and Thursday afternoons when he and his son, Jacob, 18, coach a Little League football team of fourth-, fifth- and sixth-graders.

"I love coaching those little boys," Pierce says. "My father really wasn't there for me when I was little, so I know how important it is to have a father figure. Some of the kids don't have that, and in a way I feel like I can be that for them."

FACING PAGE • As the senior control room technician at the nitration plant for the Ensign Bickford Company in Graham, Gary Pierce is in charge of operating the plant during the 7 a.m. to 3:30 p.m. shift. He checks gauges once an hour, but much of his time is spent waiting.

ABOVE • Pierce comes to life when doing something he loves to do, like coaching his football team.

AT LEFT • "It was love at first grab," says Denise Peirce, Gary's wife. As a junior in high school, Denise was walking up the stairs when Gary grabbed her behind.

THE MOUNTAIN WORKSHOPS

More than the mail

Photography by JACLYN MCCABE
Editing by JOHN BALLANCE

ABOVE • "There is a rhyme and reason to this," Terry Jessup said. "It just may not look like it." He begins work about 6:30 each morning by organizing his mail and loading the truck.

ABOVE RIGHT • Terry has been delivering mail to the same houses on the same route in Greenville for 20 years.

AS TERRY Jessup walks his route, people see a letter carrier, a man in blue pants, white shirt and blue vest. They don't see an actor rehearsing his lines for next month's Muhlenberg Community Theater production of "A Tuna Christmas."

Terry joined the U.S. Postal Service 20 years ago, and he started acting in 1983. "Everyone likes to stand up and say, 'Hey, look at me,'" he said. "My way to do that is acting."

Terry works on his lines as he walks, but his rehearsal is punctuated by the routine of his route.

On Oakview Drive, Bill McSpendden tells Terry a joke. At the Greenwood Park Apartments, Terry knows he's going to see Clifford Kirk waiting to take in mail for his neighbors. On Depot Street, Terry takes time to catch up with James Everett. He knows that Everett's dachshund, Dutch, will beg at the door until Terry arrives.

Between delivering the mail and acting, Terry finds time to care for his grandmother and to work part-time as recreation director at the Earle C. Clements Satellite Job Corps Center.

MUHLENBERG COUNTY, KENTUCKY

ABOVE • Dutch the dachshund and his owner, James Everett, wait to meet Terry every day. If he is running late, Dutch begs at the door until he arrives.

"SPOON"

Photography by **KATHLEEN COLE**
Editing by **CAROLINE E. COUIG**

WORKING, drinking, and wondering when the next good woman will come along. That's the daily routine for Bruce "Spoon" Milam.

With tattoos and a shaved head, the 32-year-old figures he's the "outlaw" at the Paradise power plant compared to his older – mostly married – co-workers.

Work is nothing but a paycheck. Happy hour at Arnett's Garage fulfills his day – especially now that his 7 1/2-year marriage is over. Spoon, his friend David Winn and whoever's not repairing a car, swap stories and "slur each other" in the back room.

After a few trips to a Pepsi machine that they've stocked with Miller Genuine Draft, Spoon admits to some regret. "I need to find me another good woman like I had."

For the married men on a wife-imposed deadline, it's dinner time. For Spoon, it's simply time to go home. Shoes off, radio on, pizza ordered, the day's almost done.

"Sometimes, I wonder why I should even come home at night – ain't nobody here but me," he says. "Just knowin' somebody was going to be here or was comin' in shortly would make me feel like a different man."

ABOVE • Spoon spends most of his days working alone on various jobs around the powerhouse. "I'm an outlaw compared to 90 percent of these guys," he says. "They think that just because I drink beer seven days a week and go to (strip clubs) every chance I get that I'm a bad person. They can say that (strip clubs) are the work of the devil, but them girls gotta make a living too."

AT LEFT • A chance meeting with ex-girlfriend Missy Randolph gives Spoon a lesson in humility. "So how is that new boy?" he asks. "Ya'll gettin' along OK living together?" Her reply: "Yeah Spoon, he's great – a whole lot better than you!"

BELOW • Spoon says if he misses the daily "happy hour" at Arnett's Garage, "something ain't right with me for days. It's religious." His buddy "Dad" David Winn, left, and Greg Polley are regular fixtures too.

THE MOUNTAIN WORKSHOPS | 71

Starting over

Photography by KATHERINE GANTER
Editing by SUSAN F.B. RYAN

MICHELLE

Stinnett wants to put her family back together.

She moved to Central City from North Carolina four months ago because things there weren't going well. After an abusive marriage, she sent her three children to live with her mother and mother-in-law in Muhlenberg County.

So Michelle got a job as a waitress at the Uptown Cafe in downtown Central City, working Thursday through Saturday from 1 p.m. to 8 p.m.

She spent her mornings performing a daily ritual of combing the classifieds for apartments. She called the Central City Housing Authority, where rent is based on income, hoping there was an opening in public housing. She got lucky.

On Thursday, Michelle signed a lease and picked up the keys to her new home. On Sunday, she and her 13-year-old son, Scott, moved into the three-bedroom duplex with her boyfriend and his son. Her mom wrote a $96 check as the down payment. Michelle's rent, in the beginning at least, will be $106 a month.

If everything goes well, her 8-year-old daughter, Samantha, will join them after the first of the year. "The big goal is to get them all back together."

Michelle's mother, Sandy Layne, is crossing her fingers. "Michelle is trying; she's doing a lot more than she's ever done."

AT LEFT • For four months, Michelle lived at home with her mother, Sandy, and her son, Scott, trying to save money. Her boyfriend and his son also moved in for a few weeks until the couple found a duplex through the city's housing authority.

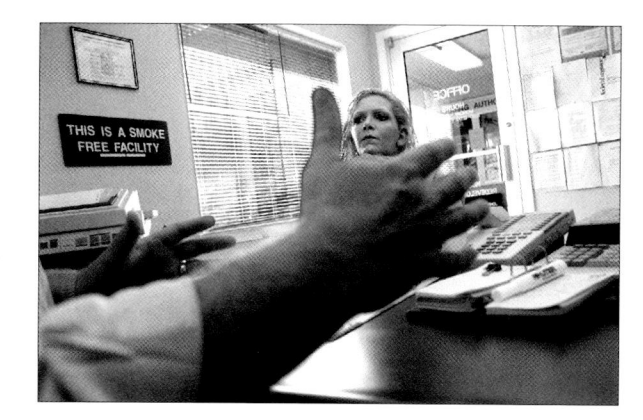

AT LEFT • Michelle is apprehensive as Johnny D. Clark, executive director of the Central City Housing Authority, addresses her concerns about how much money she will need to move in.

BELOW • After Michelle signed the papers and was given the key, she got a first look at her new home. She, her boyfriend's son, Holden, and her son, Scott (in background), listen as Martin Wallace, the housing authority's maintainance supervisor, explains how the furnace works.

THE MOUNTAIN WORKSHOPS

Starting over | continued...

"You've got to hit rock bottom before you can change. **I know what it's like to be there.** I know what it takes to get out of it."

•

Michelle Stinnett

ABOVE • Holden buttons his jacket before church one Wednesday evening.

FACING PAGE • Michelle stops in at the Uptown Cafe for a cola and a smoke as she contemplates how she's going to come up with the deposit for a new apartment.

74 | MUHLENBERG COUNTY, KENTUCKY

THE MOUNTAIN WORKSHOPS | 75

The Pickin' Place

Photography by MARK WEBER
Editing by RON GARRISON

ABOVE • Luther and Shellie Russ taught their 10 children to play music, and now on Friday nights they can listen to them play.

MUHLENBERG COUNTY, KENTUCKY

A GROUP of men

and women sit atop a homemade stage making music. Pickin' is what they call it. They play with passionate unity, the sound only a family could make. And what a family it is. Five brothers and five sisters demonstrate the skills they learned from their parents.

"Our children love playing music; we never had to make them play," says Shellie Russ, 80, as she sits on her couch beneath the family photos of her 10 children. "I would teach them three chords, and when they were ready to learn more, Luther or one of the older kids would teach them."

The love for music now brings the family together to play country music every Friday night at The Pickin' Place on their property near Central City. It is an old broken-down house on the outside. The inside is a comfortable musician's den. Christmas lights illuminate a stage on which family members play drums, piano, guitars and fiddles. Family and friends crowd together on couches to listen.

"Sometimes we have a lot of people here and sometimes we don't, sometimes we play for two hours, sometimes we play for less," says Gary, 35, the youngest of the Russ children. He'll make one guarantee: Show up at The Pickin' Place on Friday night, and there'll be music.

AT LEFT • Four generations of the Russ family make a joyful noise at their Friday jam session.

BELOW • Cheryl Russ and her daughter Rachel, 4, delight to the sounds of the family band playing in The Pickin' Place on Luther and Shellie Russ's property near Central City. Portraits of the Russ family brides hang on the wall.

Can I get a witness?

Photography by MOLLY VAN WAGNER
Editing by RON GARRISON

AT RIGHT • Otis Cunningham puts in about 40 hours a week at Woodmen of the World Insurance Company in addition to performing his responsibilities as a pastor. He says he likes insurance because of the flexibility and income. "I've got a salesman's mentality, but not a salesman's pocketbook."

BELOW • Friday night is family night at the Cunningham house. Janet, the pastor's wife, center, usually cooks a big meal — tonight it's spaghetti — and then the family plays a game. "If you don't take care of the family," Cunningham says, "then your church becomes a liability instead of an asset."

THE REV. Otis Cunningham knew he couldn't turn away when God called him to Muhlenberg County.

Fourteen years ago, Cunningham gave up financial security and risked family stability when he moved from Louisville to Central City to lead a small Southern Baptist congregation.

"We felt the Lord wanted us to come here," says Cunningham, the pastor at Ebenezer Missionary Baptist Church, a plain, steepled structure near downtown. "There was a sense of incompleteness here."

Cunningham's salary as head of a dwindling congregation isn't enough to support his family of a wife and two teen-age daughters.

"It's frustrating at times," he said, "but you feel like you make a difference helping equip people to do better."

Although he says his first responsibility is "preaching and teaching," Cunningham – known among his parishioners and colleagues as "Pastor O" – has worked as a substitute teacher, car salesman, school bus driver and lunchroom monitor.

But recently he settled on selling life insurance.

"The insurance is a ministry," Cunningham says. "You help people with their financial security through insurance."

Cunningham is almost ready to preach full-time in a larger, more profitable ministry. "We'll rejoice one day, thankful for the experiences," he says.

ABOVE • Cunningham and his wife, Janet, celebrate during a revival. "My wife is an instrumental part of the ministry, he says."

THE MOUNTAIN WORKSHOPS | 79

Rock of the spiritual community

Photography by ALAN HALE
Editing by JILL CRETSINGER

YOU could say that the Rev. Terry Groves is solid as a rock.

A pastor who pays the bills as a blaster for Hopkins County Coal works, Groves also is a down-to-earth spiritual leader.

Groves, a pastor at Freedom General Baptist Church in Graham, has been preaching since 1981.

Most of his congregation are his relatives. Many of them have the same last name. "It is what a church is supposed to be – a family," he says.

As part of his calling, he gave his own Bible to an 8-year-old parishioner who didn't have one. When she was 20, she returned the Bible. He said he cried after getting it back. He recently visited a member of his congregation in the hospital, where he was being treated for black lung.

"Brother, I know that you are suffering now but you will soon be in a place that you will suffer no more," Groves told the patient, his voice cracking.

Groves lives with his wife, Connie, in a three-room house in Graham, the town where he was born.

He says he wouldn't live anywhere else but in Muhlenburg County.

"Muhlenburg County is like a wart, it just grows on you ... this is home."

FACING PAGE • The Rev. Terry Groves, ready for church, waits for his wife.

AT LEFT • Groves prays with parishioners at the altar.

BELOW • Groves is in a rush to get out of work at a coal mine. This is a church night.

THE MOUNTAIN WORKSHOPS

Flying solo... well almost

Photography by MICHAEL BUNCH
Editing by LINDA SALAZAR

ABOVE • Charles Knight shows his excitement after having his favorite meal, hamburgers, at his brother's house.

MUHLENBERG COUNTY, KENTUCKY

EVERY DAY

is Independence Day for Charles Knight.

Charles, who just turned 52, works hard daily to cope with learning disabilities so he can live on his own. Charles, nicknamed "Witty" by his friends and family, experienced severe seizures as a child. He's been on his own since his father died in 1979. His older brother, Tommy, bought Charles a trailer that sits on Tommy's property about 30 yards from his brother's home.

"We taught him to mop and clean, and now he pretty much takes care of himself," Tommy says.

He works at the Muhlenberg Opportunity Center five days a week, packaging screws and plastic pieces for mini-blinds. He's been there 30 years. The center employs mentally and physically challenged invuduals. It matches a job with a person's ability.

On weeknights, Charles dines with his family. He prefers to spend his time quietly, watching TV or listening to gospel music. He attends church services on Wednesday and Sunday and rarely misses a revival.

"The people in the church have taken him in," Tommy says. "A lot of people show interest in him."

AT LEFT • Every weekday morning and afternoon, Knight, center, rides the Opportunity Center bus to work.

BELOW • A great deal of Knight's time is spent alone at his trailer. He watches the news every morning and listens to one of his many gospel cassettes to begin his day.

THE MOUNTAIN WORKSHOPS | 83

With a little help from my friends

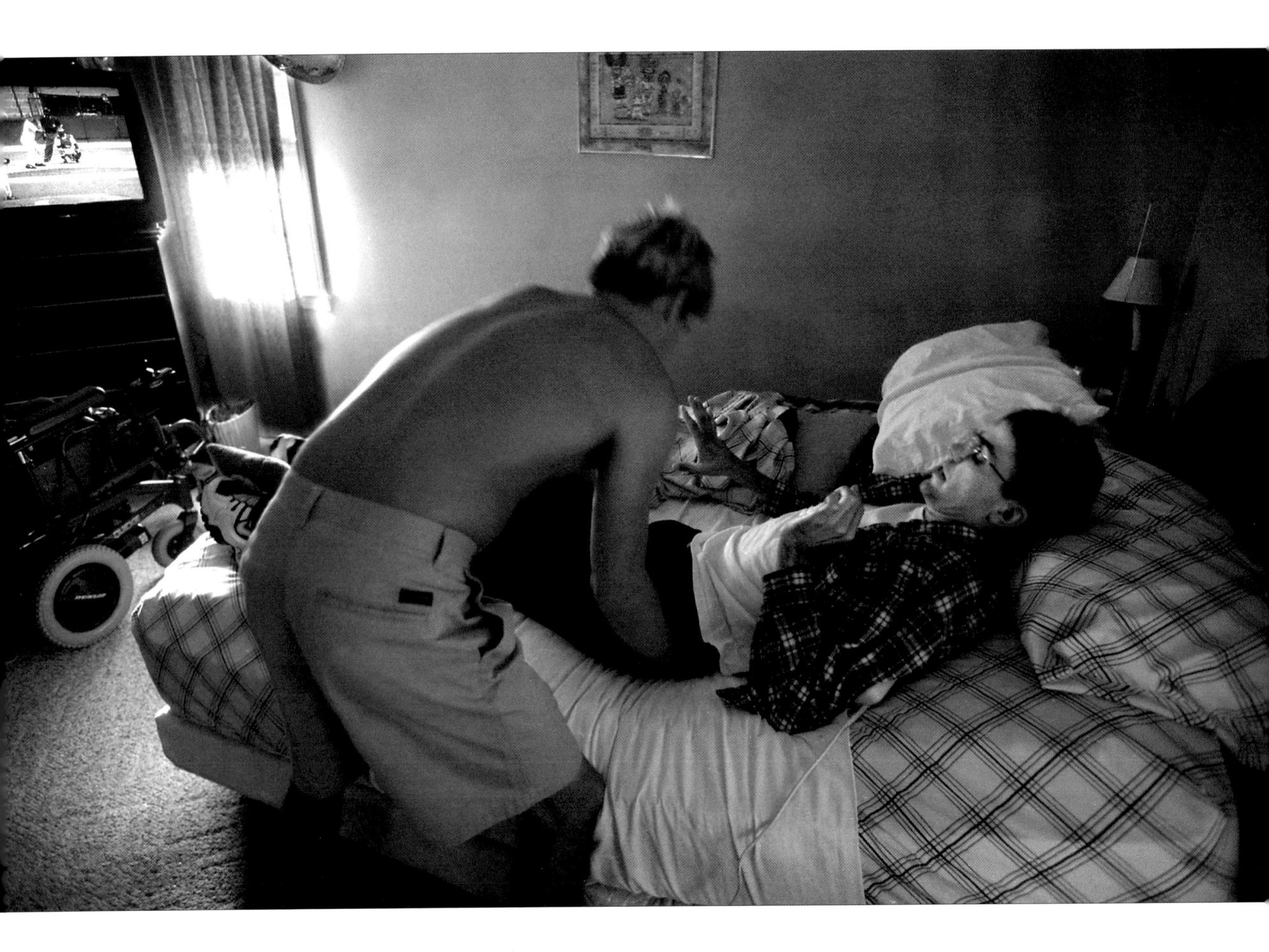

Photography by JUSTIN RUMBACH
Editing by CAROLINE E. COUIG

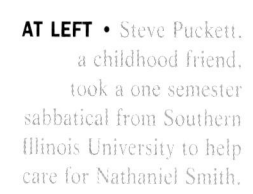

AT LEFT • Steve Puckett, a childhood friend, took a one semester sabbatical from Southern Illinois University to help care for Nathaniel Smith.

AT RIGHT • Nathaniel, his girlfriend Angie and their daughter Paige talk about their day before going to bed. Nathaniel says the worst repercussion from his accident is not being able to hold his daughter. "I am determined," he said, "to be able to walk Paige down the aisle to give her away on her wedding day."

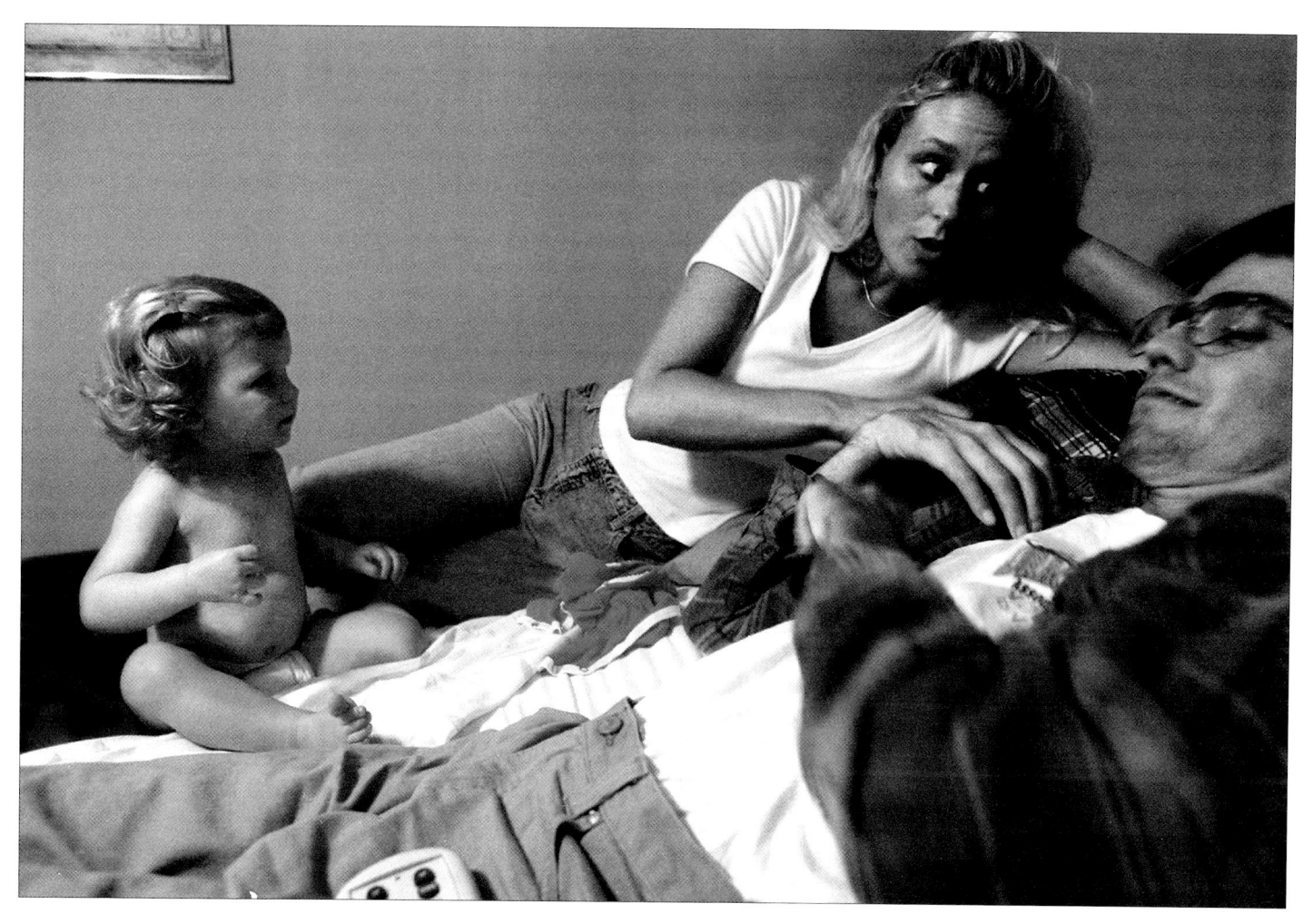

FRIENDS don't let friends drive drunk. So on May 5, 1999, Nathaniel Smith drove a drunk friend home.

But in the pelting rain, he lost control of the Toyota pickup and hit an embankment, rolling the truck.

His friend walked away. Nathaniel is now confined to a wheelchair – no feeling from the waist down. Getting dressed takes two hours. A friend has to hold his cigarettes up to his mouth.

"I didn't know, when I saw people in wheelchairs, that they went through this much hell," the 24-year-old said. "I'd do anything to have just a couple of broken legs and ribs."

His relationships have changed surprisingly little. Every day, his girlfriend of seven years, Angie Vincent, stops by with their 17-month-old daughter, Paige. The three spend a lot of time cuddling in bed. "That's the thing that bothers him the most – not being able to hold his daughter," Angie said.

Childhood friend Steve Puckett took a semester off from college to help out.

And Shawn Clemens often swings by to get Nathaniel out of the house. He just picks Nathaniel out of his wheelchair and puts him into the truck.

"This is the true test," Nathaniel said. "When something like this happens you find out who your real friends are."

THE MOUNTAIN WORKSHOPS | 85

With a little help from my friends | continued...

AT RIGHT • Nathaniel has his blood checked monthly to ensure that his medications, which include more than 40 pills a day, aren't affecting his liver. Even though he doesn't have much feeling in his extremities, he said he has always been afraid of getting shots.

BELOW • Nathaniel's first visit to the Riverpark Health Center in Owensboro, Ky., was exhausting. He makes the 70-mile round trip from Central City three times a week because he can get more intensive therapy than is available at home.

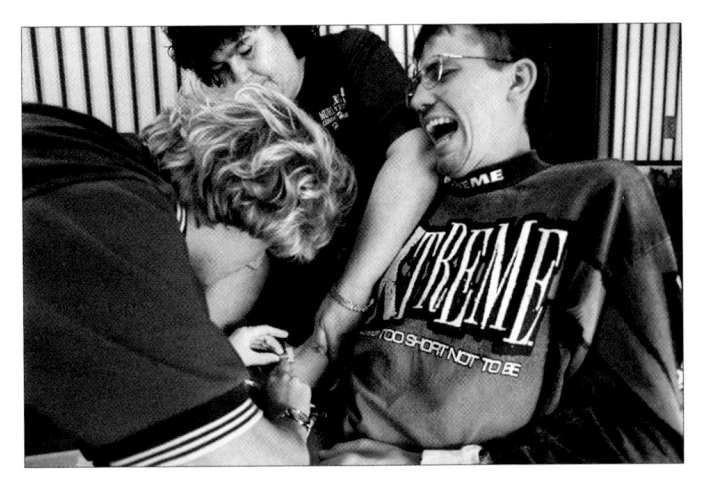

ABOVE • Nathaniel's long-time friend, J.R. Hardison, tries to annoy Nathaniel by flirting with his girlfriend, Angie. Nathaniel says getting out of the house and hanging out with friends makes him feel more normal.

Closing time at Cohen & Son

Photography by CARA VANLEUVEN
Editing by STACY HAYES

IN 1909, a Jewish man named Edward Alec Cohen settled his family in Greenville and started a small dry goods store on South Main Street. It thrived, supporting a family and a town.

"The saying around here was if you can't find it anyplace else, it's at Cohen's," Greenville native Fred Geibel recalls.

Edward came to Muhlenberg County from Poland in 1905, traveling from town to town, selling goods off his back. After four years, he had enough money to start a store.

People still remember that during the Depression, the store gave credit. By 1946, the post-war boom lifted Muhlenberg County. The name of the store was changed from E. A. Cohen to E. A. Cohen & Son, and Julius, the only son of six children, was asked by his dad to help manage.

Julius was behind the cash register, helping customers find the otherwise hard-to-find, until he was 83. But by 1999, his children had moved away, his wife had died. It was time to retire.

FACING PAGE • Nearly four months after Cohen's closed, it still was not empty. Julius walks out after removing a framed picture that hung on the wall. In October, light fixtures, bottles and an antique organ that didn't work were still for sale.

ABOVE • E.A. Cohen & Son started as a small dry goods store in 1909 and expanded to take up storefronts stretching nearly an entire block on South Main Street in Greenville. They included a hardware store, a furniture store and a general store. Here, Julius locks the door of the main entrance after a brief visit.

THE MOUNTAIN WORKSHOPS

Closing time at Cohen & Son | continued...

E.A. Cohen & Son was **a feed store, grocery store and hardware store,** sometimes all at once. It grew from a single storefront to the length of an entire block.

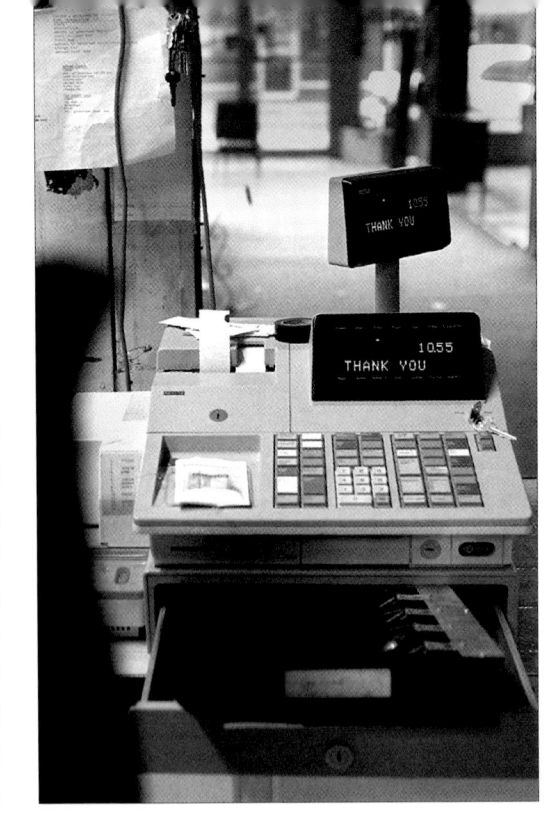

AT LEFT • Julius was 83 when he last stood behind the register counter at E. A. Cohen & Son.

AT RIGHT • After eating lunch, reading the paper and getting the score of a baseball game, Julius dozes off. His afternoons were spent shelving stock and delivering goods for 53 years. "I wish I had retired about 10 years ago. I'd be in better shape to enjoy it," Julius said.

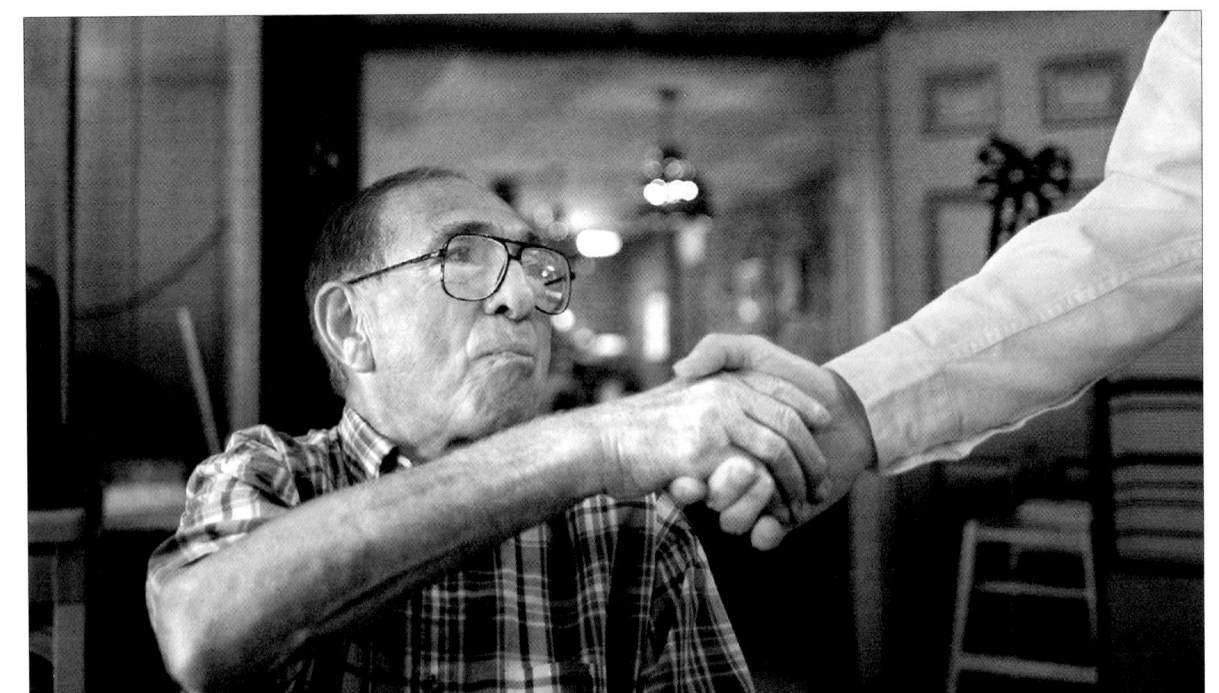

AT LEFT • Julius greets old friend Fred Geibel at the Family Inn, a downtown restaurant. He can't go anywhere in downtown Greenville without having someone come up to say hello. But he's part of a diminishing group. Muhlenberg County was once home to 12 Jewish families, but by the end of 1999, there were only 10 Jews in the county. They once worshipped in a synagogue in nearby Hopkinsville that's now the site of a used car lot.

90 | MUHLENBERG COUNTY, KENTUCKY

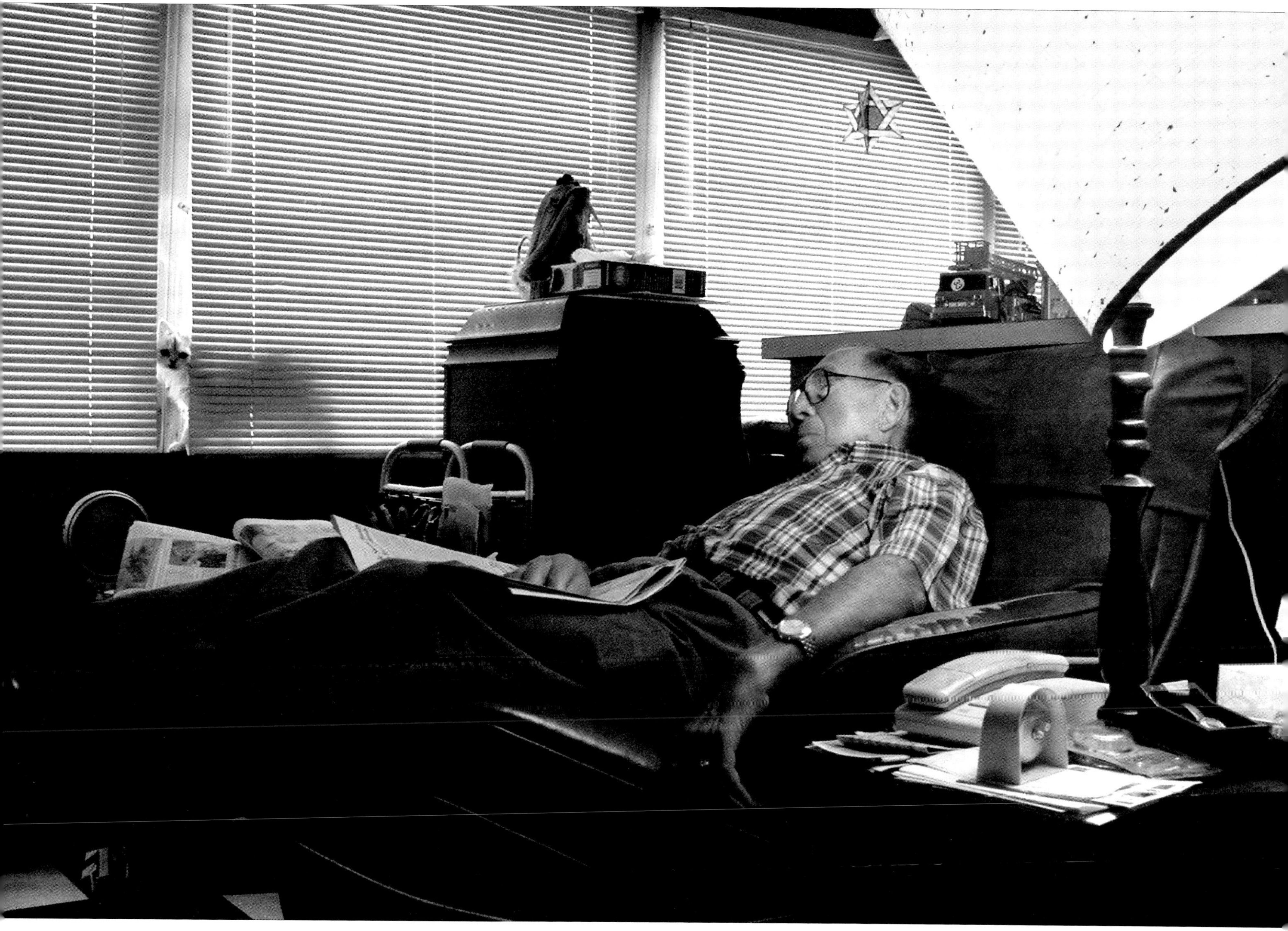

Friday night hero

Photography by NEAL CARDIN
Editing by LINDA SALAZAR

AT RIGHT • On a wet Friday night, Joey Mercer gained nearly 300 yards, leading his team to its second victory.

BELOW • Joey chats with teammates after the game against the Grayson County Cougars.

JOEY Mercer sits on a bench, leaning his head against a locker. His hands are clasped, fingers interlocked. He has his poker face on. His teammates joke and fuss with their football uniforms. It's time for the Stars to play their seventh game of the season.

The team is 1-5. Joey worries that playing for a team with such a poor record limits his exposure to scouts. His parents feel that way, too.

"I hate it," his mother, Debbie says. "He can't show what he could do."

Joey, 18, a senior at Muhlenberg North High School, is the "iron man" of the team. The 5-foot-9-inch 175-pounder plays offense and defense.

"I come off the field two times in the game," he said after practice. "Once at half time and the other is at the end of the fourth quarter."

But one rainy Friday night in October, his luck improved. The Stars defeated the Grayson County Cougars, 26-10, bringing their record to 2-5. Before the game the team had 12 touchdowns, nine of those by Joey.

Joey rushed for almost 300 yards that Friday, for a total of 1,000 yards in the season.

"He takes about 4,000 hits a game," said teammate Scott Young. "I don't see how he lives."

MUHLENBERG COUNTY, KENTUCKY

ABOVE • Joey and Sarah Everly stop for a hot fudge sundae at the Dairy Freeze.

THE MOUNTAIN WORKSHOPS | 93

Birth of a new father

Photography by TOM LEININGER
Editing by KATHY WILCUTT COWAN

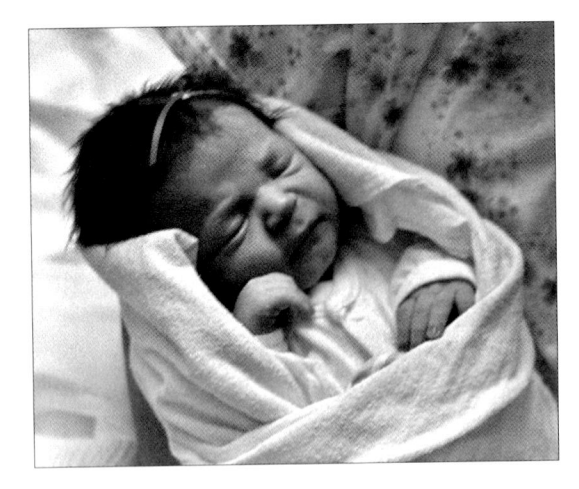

PHILLIP Hines, 21, became a father at 5:36 a.m. on Tuesday, Oct. 5, 1999, at the Muhlenberg Community Hospital. His daughter, Haley Lynn Hines, 9 pounds 7 ounces, 19 1/2 inches, entered the world with a head full of her dad's black hair.

"People say she looks like me," Hines says. "But she is much prettier."

Phil and Jennifer plan to get married soon. They are working on an addition to their house in Lewisburg and adjusting to having another child. Jennifer Crowder already has three children, Kevin, 9, Ashley, 4, and Kaitlyn, 18 months.

Sitting on the couch in their house, holding his new daughter, he presses her nose and plays with her hands.

"I makes me feel good...It's like I had a part in creating something."

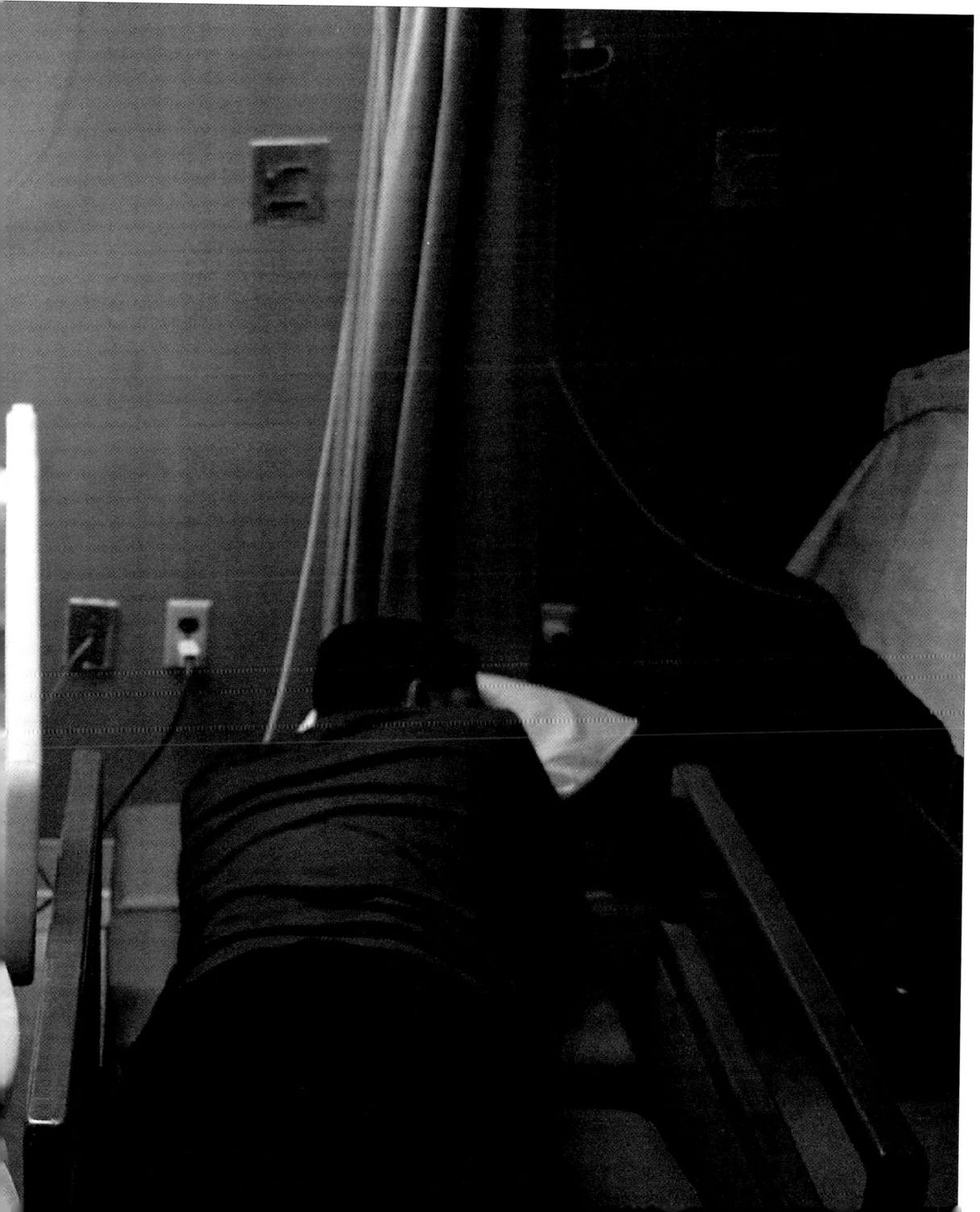

"People say she **looks like me,** but she is much prettier."

•

new father Philip Hines

ABOVE • Jennifer and fiancé Phil try to get comfortable in bed with their daughters Haley and Kaitlyn in their Lewisburg home.

AT LEFT • Phil takes a nap after the birth of his daughter while his fiancée, Jennifer, holds the newborn.

A picture of this large gang and a litany of our history...

AT RIGHT • Mountain Workshop participants gather for the annual group photograph in the drill hall at Wendell H. Ford Regional Training Center. The hall was the venue for daily story critiques and presentations by the faculty.

The 1999 Mountain Workshop group photos

#1 • *1976 / One-room schools*
#2 • *1977 / Main Street*
#3 • *1978 / LBL, Kentucky*
#4 • *1979 / Clairfield, Tenn.*
#5 • *1980 / Burkesville, Ky.*
#6 • *1981 / Burkesville, Ky.*
#7 • *1982 / Tompkinsville, Ky.*
#8 • *1983 / Morgantown, Ky.*
#9 • *1984 / Celina, Tenn.*
#10 • *1985 / Edmonton, Ky*
#11 • *1986 / Scottsville, Ky.*
#12 • *1987 / Liberty, Ky.*
#13 • *1988 / Russell Springs, Ky.*
#14 • *1989 / Albany, Ky.*
#15 • *1990 / Monticello, Ky.*
#16 • *1991 / Lafayette, Tenn.*
#17 • *1992 / Columbia, Ky.*
#18 • *1993 / Jamestown, Tenn.*
#19 • *1994 / Glasgow, Ky.*
#20 • *1995 / Smithville, Tenn.*
#21 • *1996 / Campbellsville, Ky*
#22 • *1997 / Russellville, Ky.*
#23 • *1998 / Franklin, Ky.*
#24 • *1998 / Central City, Ky.*

ABOVE • Luck has a lot to do with the assignment process at the Mountain Workshops. Here, participants Jonathan Kirshner, left, Kathleen Flynn, center, and Amber Woolfolk pick their story assignments from a hat held by faculty member Susie Post. (Robin Buckson photos)

MUHLENBERG COUNTY, KENTUCKY

THE MOUNTAIN WORKSHOPS | 97

Cast of Characters

All the folks who came to Muhlenberg County

All special thanks to these folks:

- Francis Gardler, *Patuxent Publishing*
- Greg Lamb, *Studio III*

PHOTO EQUIPMENT SUPPORT

Tom Bullington
Canon U.S.A. Inc.
Robert J. Luce & Steve Carlisle
Fuji Photo Film U.S.A. Inc.
Fred Sisson
Nikon Inc.

SPONSORS

- The Photojournalism Foundation Inc.
- Fuji Photo Film U.S.A. Inc.
- Western Kentucky University
- Nikon Inc.
- Canon U.S.A. Inc.
- Photofax
- The Software Construction Co.
- Phrasea/Baseview-Intl.
- The John S. and James L. Knight Foundation
- Photo Systems Inc.
- Marantz Professional Audio
- Apple Computer
- Lazer-Fare Media Services
- B & L Parenthesis
- Pinnacle Technologies Inc.
- Sony Corp.
- The Muhlenburg County Chamber of Commerce
- The Central City Chamber of Commerce

Photos on this page by Robin Buckson

This year's workshop participants:

PHOTOGRAPHERS

Mark Andrews, *Western Kentucky University* • **Seshu Badrinath**, *Ohio University* •
Stuart Bauer, *The Flint Journal* • **Shayna C. Breslin**, *Western Kentucky University* •
Michael Bunch, *Western Kentucky University* • **Steven Buyansky**, *The Beacon News* •
George Callender, *Virginia Beach, Virginia* • **Neal Cardin**, *News Enterprise* •
Jahi Chikwendiu, *Lexington Herald-Leader* • **Kathleen Cole**, *University of Georgia* •
Paul Conrad, *Western Kentucky University* • **Thomas Cordy**, *Western Kentucky University* •
Miranda Ellis, *Western Kentucky University* • **Suzanne Feliciano**, *The State Journal* •
Kathleen Flynn, *Western Kentucky University* • **Katherine Ganter**, *The Alexandria Daily Town Talk* •
Alan Hale, *Western Kentucky University* • **Mark Hendengren**, *Deseret News* •
Christie House, *New World Outlook* • **Ethan Hyman**, *The Post Bulletin* • **Lawrence Jackson**, *The Virginian Pilot* •
Terrence James, *Chicago Tribune* • **J. Mark Kegans**, *Arlington Morning News* •
Melanie Kimbler, *Western Kentucky University* • **Krystal Kinnunen**, *Western Kentucky University* •
Jonathan Kirshner, *Western Kentucky University* • **Lisa Krantz**, *Naples Daily News* •
Robyn Larsen, *Western Kentucky University* • **Tom Leininger**, *The Journal and Courier* •
Dawn Majors, *Western Kentucky University* • **Jaclyn McCabe**, *Western Kentucky University* •
M.J. McDonald, *Western Kentucky University* • **Jonathan Meester**, *University of Iowa* •
Terri Miller, *Western Kentucky University* • **Cory Mitchell**, *Western Kentucky University* •
Judi Parks, *Oakland, California* • **Andrew Otto**, *Western Kentucky University* •
Sarah Reingewirtz, *The Bakersfield Californian* • **Justin Rumbach**, *The Evansville Press* •
James Sands, *The Herald Dispatch* • **Kyung Sook Schoenman**, *University of Kentucky* •
Jill Snyder, *Western Kentucky University* • **Chad Stevens**, *Western Kentucky University* •
Shawn Thew, *Silver Spring, Maryland.* • **Molly Van Wagner**, *University of Florida* •
Cara VanLeuven, *Western Kentucky University* • **Daniel Wallace**, *Western Kentucky University* •
Mark Weber, *Western Kentucky University* • **Amber Woolfolk**, *Western Kentucky University*

PICTURE EDITORS

John Ballance, *The Advocate* • **Jill Cretsinger**, *Oshkosh Northwestern* •
Caroline E. Couig, *The Detroit Free Press* • **Kathy Cowan**, *The News Democrat and Leader* •
Amy Deputy, *The Baltimore Sun* • **Stacy Hayes**, *Western Kentucky University* •
Ron Garrison, *Lexington Herald-Leader* • **Jose R. Lopez**, *The New York Times* •
Nerissa Miller, *Western Kentucky University* • **Susan F.B. Ryan**, *St. Louis Post-Dispatch* •
Linda Salazar, *The Arizona Daily Star*

Mike Morse, Workshop Director

Steve Mellon, Pittsburg Post-Gazette

Kenny Irby, The Poynter Institute

Mike Smith, The New York Times

Larry Powell, Freelance

MUHLENBERG COUNTY, KENTUCKY

This year's workshop staff, faculty and special helpers

Paula Nelson, The Dallas Morning News

Susan Gilbert, The Charlotte Observer

Janet Reeves, Rocky Mountain News

Michael Williamson, Washington Post

Robin Buckson, The Detroit News

The Workshop Directors

Mike Morse
*Workshop Director,
Western Kentucky University*
James Kenney
Workshop Imaging Team Coordinator, WKU
Susie Post
Story Coordinator, WKU
Tim Broekema
*Multimedia/Audio Visual Coordinator,
The Kalamazoo Gazette*

The Photo Faculty

Joe Elbert
The Washington Post
John Davidson
The Dallas Morning News
Susan Gilbert
The Charlotte Observer
Bill Greene
The Boston Globe
Kenny Irby
The Poynter Institute for Media Studies
Steve Mellon
The Pittsburgh Post-Gazette
Michael Williamason
The Washington Post
Janet Reeves
Rocky Mountain News

The Picture Editing Faculty

Randy Cox
The Oregonian
Mark Edelson
The Palm Beach Post
Lynette Holman
Birmingham Post-Herald
Paula Nelson
The Dallas Morning News
Scott Sines
The Spokesman-Review
Mike Smith
The New York Times

The Writing Faculty

Harry Allen
*Western Kentucky University
Writing Coordinator*
Suzan Bibisi
The Waterbury Republican-American
Tom Eblen
Lexington Herald-Leader
Richard Hart
Raleigh News and Observer
Cynthia Mitchell
Atlanta, Georgia
Tom O'Neill
National Geographic

The Workshop Staff

Robin Buckson
*The Detroit News
Workshop Photojournalist*
Kim Hughes
*The Idaho Statesman
Assistant to the Director*
Jonathan Newton
*The Washington Post
Lab Director*
Larry Powell
*Freelance
Logistics Coordinator*
Toni Sandys
*St. Petersburg Times
Imaging Team*

Imaging Team

John Dunham
The Messenger-Inquirer
Fran Gardler
Patuxent Publishing Company
Amy Smotherman
South Bend Tribune

New Media and Technology Staff

Bob Bruck
*The Messenger-Inquirer
Multimedia Assistant*
Wes Burcham
*Photo Systems Inc.
Network Systems Manager*
Mike Curlett
*Photo Systems Inc.
Network Systems Associate*
Bruce Ely
*The Evansville Press
Web Team*
Carl Ganter
MediaVia LLC

Audio Editor

Eileen Ganter
*MediaVia LLC
Audio Editor*
Ken Harper
*Arizona Daily Star
Web Team*
Shane Iseminger
*Ethos Media
CD Rom Coordinator*
Jeff Martin
*Western Kentucky University
Network Stystems Associate*
Brian Masck
*The Flint Journal
Electronics Coordinator*

1999 Labbies

Mark Anderson, Nathaniel Corn, Katie Englert, Ruth Kennedy, Jeremy Lyverse, Rick Mach, Amanda Mauer, Carisa McCain, Chris Moore, Denise Muschel, Sean Payne, Brian Pierro, Shawn Poynter, Megan Resch, Karl Schmidt, Jonny Sevcik, Walter Smith Wendi Thompson, Valerie Tobias, Robyn Wade, Guy Wathen, Estelle Williams, Yuli Wu

Copy Editor

Corban "Hawkeye" Goble
Western Kentucky University, Retired

Web Site

http://www.mountainworkshops.org

An Epilogue

"If you're open and honest up front, most people will let you into their life..."

ON TUESDAY, they were strips of white paper with the barest of information. A name. A phone number. A line of description — two or three lines at most.

By Saturday, 50 shooters and 11 photo editors had turned those ideas into full-blown photo stories — clusters of images and words that, together, framed windows into the soul of this rural Kentucky county.

But the journey from Tuesday to Saturday was no straight line. The "older fella that runs a junk yard," whom Lisa Krantz drew as her assignment from the gimme cap, didn't want to be photographed. Instead, she mustered the courage to befriend a group of teen-age boys. What she caught on film prompted a provocative debate in that night's critique. When do you shoot now and ask questions later? When do you put down your camera?

Kathleen Cole's strip of paper read: "Place with the huge Three Mile Island-looking smoke stacks. Need to find someone there to photograph." She found a walking contradiction named Bruce "Spoon" Milam. He was indeed the beer-drinking bachelor he first claimed to be. But Cole, a University of Georgia senior, peeled back the bravado to find a heartsick romantic who had picked out two Shania Twain songs for his next wedding.

Even the "fish in a barrel" stories weren't necessarily so easy. Shayna Breslin figured on chaos when she drew the assignment: "Tony Daniel. Family with lots of kids." She found a couple of devout Pentecostals with 11 children at home who weren't sure their biblical charge to "live simply" included having their lives documented on film. "We'll let you know tomorrow," they told her Tuesday afternoon, adding that she was welcome to join them for church. After the three-hour service, they asked her home and told her she could sleep in one of the kids' rooms.

To get all of those scenes from camera to classroom, Brian Masck, Jeff Martin, Wes Burcham and James Kenney masterminded a network of 60 computers. More than 18,000 photographic images and sound bites – representing 22 gigabytes of data — were scanned into computers by the "Labbies," 26 Western Kentucky University students recognizable by their hand-drawn "Labbie Love" arm tattoos and their sleep-starved punchiness.

Speaking of which...

Almost every shooter was up at dawn at least once, trying to grab that "magic light" that comes just after sunrise. For many, there wasn't a choice. Krystal Kinnunen's subject, Judy Higgs, the cook at the Green River Correctional Complex, reported to work at 3:30 a.m. Jonathan Kirshner's alarm went off at 5 a.m. every morning, but the best light the WKU student could hope for was from the miners' headlamps inside the Paradise No. 9 Mine.

The early risers didn't get a break. The nightly slide shows and critiques rarely wrapped up before 11 p.m. After that, the photo coaches kept their teams clustered around computers, discussing each shooter's images and helping them discern what they had and what they lacked. After that, the writing room usually filled up. After that, it was time for what workshop director Mike Morse liked to call, "the unofficial debriefing."

For Steve Buyansky, a photographer at The Beacon News in Aurora, Ill., turning that white slip into a real-live human being taught him lessons in overcoming stereotypes and initial jitters. His slip read: "Royce Morgan, thumbpicker." He conjured up the stereotype of a grizzled old man in a hillbilly shack, picking his guitar. Turned out Morgan had a storied career in the music business, a thriving farm and a Cadillac parked in his garage.

"It's kind of like asking a girl out — the fear of failure is sort of the same thing," Buyansky said. "After this workshop and a little experience, I know if they say no, they say no, but most likely most people will say yes. If you're open and honest up front, most people will let you into their life."

• *Cynthia Mitchell*
Freelance Writer

ABOVE • A miner borrowed the camera of workshop participant Jonathan Kirshner to make this picture of the WKU student being "spanked" with hammers at Paradise No. 9. It was Kirshner's 22nd birthday.

MUHLENBERG COUNTY, KENTUCKY